Contribut

Dean Baker is the co-direc
the Center for Economic and Policy
Research.

Joanne Barkan is a writer who
lives in Manhattan and Truro,
Massachusetts.

Megan Erickson is an editor at
Jacobin. She taught reading and
writing to ninth and tenth graders in
New York City public schools.

Remeike Forbes is the creative
director of *Jacobin*.

Shawn Gude is associate editor
at *Jacobin*.

Andrew Hartman teaches history
at Illinois State University.
He is the author of *Education
and the Cold War: The Battle for
the American School*.

Adam Heenan is a high school
social studies teacher and education
activist. He is currently in his ninth
year and is an elected delegate to the
Chicago Teachers Union.

Will Johnson is a special education
teacher in New York City.

Mariame Kaba is an organizer,
educator, and writer who lives in
Chicago. She is the founder and
director of Project NIA, a grassroots
organization with a mission to end
youth incarceration.

Karen Lewis is the president of the
Chicago Teachers Union.

Erica R. Meiners is a professor of
gender and women's studies and
education at Northeastern Illinois
University. She is the author of
several books, including *Flaunt
It! Queers Organizing for Public
Education and Justice*.

Katrina Ohstrom is a Philadelphia-
based photographer and activist.

Kevin Prosen is a chapter leader in
the United Federation of Teachers
and a member of the Movement of
Rank-and-File Educators, the social
justice caucus of the UFT.

Kenzo Shibata was a founding
member and former communications
director for CORE and is currently
a digital media strategist, writer, and
educator.

Bhaskar Sunkara is the founding
editor of *Jacobin*.

Micah Uetricht is the online editor
of *Jacobin* and the author of
*Strike for America: Chicago Teachers
Against Austerity*.

Lois Weiner is a professor of
education at New Jersey City
University and is on the editorial
board of *New Politics*. Her newest
book is *The Future of Our Schools:
Teachers Unions and Social Justice*.

Contents

Saving
Our Schools

From the beginning, *Jacobin* has paid special attention to the struggle of public workers against unrelenting budget cuts. The magazine's critiques of neoliberal education reform have been the centerpiece of this effort — with our work penetrating into mainstream venues like the *Washington Post* and Salon and helping to change the conversation about American schools.

The focus was justified. With so much of the education reform movement's impetus coming from liberals, communities resisting the push have been left with few allies. As a publication that has a young core audience, we thought it important to make clear that K-12 education issues are salient to everyone, not just teachers, students, and parents. That meant connecting the education "reform" project specifically to the larger trend towards market solutions as an orienting vision — not just for the schools but for society as a whole.

American public schools are increasingly seen by politicians, business people, and philanthropists as a sorting facility where children either seize opportunity or surrender it. Education "reformers" like Michelle Rhee and Joel Klein rhetorically connect standards and accountability to egalitarianism, using liberal language to advocate for a radically conservative reform agenda which consists of union busting, merit pay, and school privatization.

But with the emergence of a new movement against corporate education reform, most significantly with the 2012 Chicago Teachers Union strike, we saw signs of what can happen when teachers and their allies unite to resist this agenda and present visions of an alternative. In turn, *Jacobin* articles like "Lean Production" received a wide audience among teachers in Chicago and beyond. Our partnership with the CTU's Caucus of Rank and File Educators comes from this exchange.

This booklet is meant to be useful to those engaged in struggle — used for tabling and flyering, fuel for reading groups and public debate. The vast majority is written by current or former educators from Chicago, New York, and elsewhere. We hope this modest contribution will help to show not just the perniciousness of budget cuts, but its connection to a broader corporate offensive on our communities.

A high-quality education system that's equal and democratic, safe streets on which to play and grow into maturity, freedom from the blight of poverty — these are the birthright of every child. Corporate reformers can't offer them such a future. Now more than ever, educators have a central role in building an alternative that does.

In the summer of 2013 Chicago shut down 49 of its schools in the largest single wave of public school closures in history. Katrina Ohstrom set out to document the fate of these schools soon after the closures.

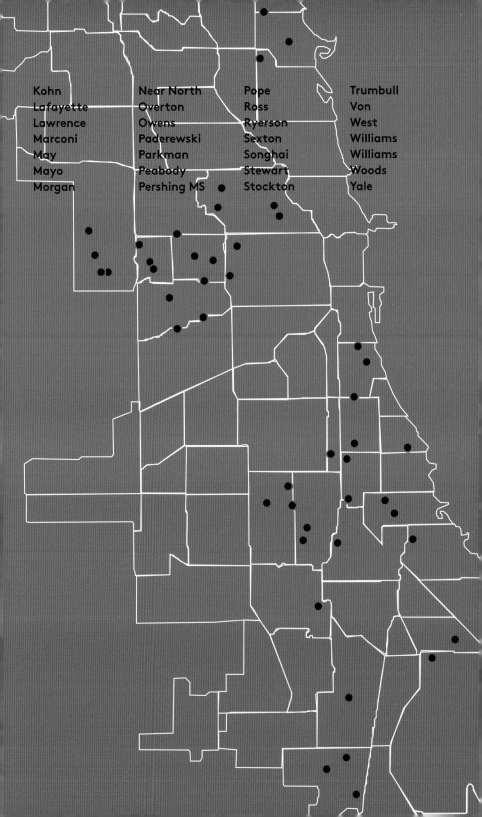

Kohn
Lafayette
Lawrence
Marconi
May
Mayo
Morgan

Near North
Overton
Owens
Paderewski
Parkman
Peabody
Pershing MS

Pope
Ross
Ryerson
Sexton
Songhai
Stewart
Stockton

Trumbull
Von
West
Williams
Williams
Woods
Yale

The Industrial Classroom

The goal of lean education isn't teaching or learning. It's creating lean workplaces where teachers are stretched to their limits.

Lean
Production

WILL JOHNSON

I n September 2012, nearly 30,000 Chicago teachers went on strike for the first time in 25 years. This was no mere breakdown in negotiations over wages or healthcare contributions. At issue, as many have noted, was the fundamental direction of public education. The Chicago teachers asserted themselves as the first institutional force to combat what's often called the "business model" of education reform.

Meanwhile, in Detroit, students and teachers returned to dramatically altered schools. Over the summer, Roy Roberts, the schools' "emergency financial manager," had unilaterally imposed a contract on the city's teachers' union allowing elementary school class sizes to jump from 25 to 40 students and high school classes to 61 students. These class size reforms were coupled with a 10% pay cut for Detroit teachers.

While Detroit's example is extreme, increased workloads for decreased pay are what teachers around the country — including in Chicago — are experiencing to varying degrees as the business model of education reform gains traction with policy-makers. But stretching workers past their breaking point and increasing hours while gutting compensation is nothing new. The business model of education reform is an extension of a process called lean production that transformed the US private sector in the 1980s and 1990s. In education, just as in heavy manufacturing, the greatest damage done by lean production is not done at the bargaining table, but in the destruction of teachers' working (and students' learning) conditions.

The Team Concept

My first two years teaching in New York City, I worked at an exemplary "lean" high school. This school twice received "A" ratings on its progress reports from the Department of Education, and it was rated "well developed" (the highest possible rating) in a 2011 quality review. Curiously, my former school's stellar ratings were awarded despite its poor academic record, itself a matter of public record (see below).

When the Department of Education wrote its "quality review" of my former school, the first set of commendations focused on the administration's use of teams. "The principal," the report reads, "promotes organizational decisions ... through a distributive team leadership model that consistently improve instruction and student outcomes." Basically, my principal was being lauded for putting teachers on lots of different teams and giving those teams lots of responsibilities.

At first, being on teams sounds like fun. Teachers at my old school worked on grade teams, department teams, inquiry teams, "case-conferencing teacher teams," and "'Teachers as Critical Friends' groups." All teachers attended three staff meetings per week, often breaking into small teams — per the administration's instructions. But based on this school's academic failures, these teams clearly weren't leading to "improved student outcomes." So why was the Department of Education so happy about them?

The team concept is a critical component of lean production. In lean workplaces, labor journalist Jane Slaughter writes, worker teams are designed to enlist workers "in speeding up their own jobs…. It is no longer enough for workers to come to work and do their jobs; they need to become 'partners in production.'"

School managers promote teams as empowering for teachers; according to management, they give teachers a say in how their schools are run. In reality, these meetings highlight how little control teachers have over their time and workload at lean schools. Morning meetings can be particularly miserable, as teachers desperate for preparation time are forced to sit through an agenda focused on management concerns. In fact, the apparent purpose of teacher teams is to shift administrative workload onto teachers.

At my former school, for example, faculty teams were tasked with designing the rubric our principal would use to evaluate our teaching; case-conferencing teams were tasked with establishing flexible disciplinary systems so that our administration would not have to discipline difficult students; and grade teams were tasked with organizing school events, like field trips and parties. These tasks were piled on top of teaching workloads that were constantly increasing due to growing class sizes and cuts to support staff. Teachers at lean schools are stretched to their limits. This is not an accident.

The team concept both increases stress on the workforce and creates the illusion that workers themselves are responsible for this stress. After all, the teacher teams assign themselves the work. Of course, in a lean school, teachers are never given the option to reject the team model, which generates the work; they have to choose between being a "team player" and volunteering for new tasks and responsibilities or letting down their coworkers.

The cumulative result is, predictably, frustration and exhaustion: frustration because teachers constantly find themselves having to shortchange their pedagogical responsibilities (planning lessons, developing curricula) and focus on team (administrative) responsibilities; and exhaustion because teacher workloads were barely manageable before this additional work was assigned.

The Industrial Classroom

The name "lean production" suggests that the practice emphasizes ruthless efficiency and eliminating waste. True, but those tactics have been around since the Industrial Revolution. What makes lean production unique from other forms of capitalist production is its "Management by Stress" approach: to achieve maximum efficiency, management deliberately stresses workplace systems to the point of breakdown.

In Choosing Sides: Unions and the Team Concept, Jane Slaughter and Mike Parker note that production in US factories was traditionally supposed to keep moving 24/7. Breakdowns were considered crises. In a lean factory, however, supervisors speed up the production process until a worker drops a widget, loses a finger, or has a nervous breakdown. Such breakdowns are viewed as a positive because they allow management to identify weak links in the chain of production. As Slaughter and Parker write, "If the system is stressed ... the weakest points become evident.... Once the problems have been corrected, the system can then be further stressed (perhaps by reducing the number of workers) and then rebalanced." The line can then be sped up again until the next breakdown occurs.

Occupational stress and its attendant physical and mental breakdowns have always been risks for teachers, but in lean schools, such breakdowns are a management goal. The consequences for teachers and students are catastrophic. Not surprisingly, teacher turnover rates have increased dramatically as schools have gotten leaner and leaner. *USA Today* recently reported that the average classroom teacher now has one year of experience. Research indicates that turnover is 50 percent higher in high-poverty schools — which happen to be the laboratories for lean production in education — than affluent ones.

Day to day, high turnover hurts staff cohesion and the shared sense of community in schools. A recent

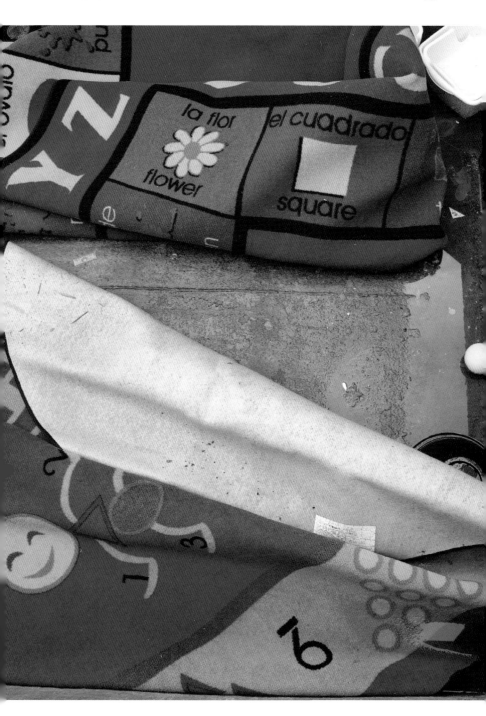

study conducted by researchers from the University of Michigan, Stanford, and the University of Virginia found that teacher turnover even takes an academic toll on students. The researchers found that an increase in teacher turnover "by 1 standard deviation corresponded with a decrease in math achievement of 2 percent of a standard deviation."

The predictable increase in teacher turnover reflects another hallmark of lean production: replacing skilled workers with an unskilled, contingent workforce. Despite a wealth of research showing that students fare better with experienced teachers, advocates of lean education from New York City Mayor Mike Bloomberg to Teach for America CEO Wendy Kopp advocate programs (like TFA) that place inexperienced, poorly trained teachers in classrooms for 1–3 years, burn them out, and replace them with a new batch. In lean education, teaching becomes a low-skilled, temporary job, regardless of how turnover affects students and schools.

Value Added Assessment

Another hallmark of lean production that's made its way into public schools is value added assessment. The concept emerged from the lean technique of value mapping, wherein managers track the flow of value through each stage of the production process. In a lean workplace, the ideal is an unobstructed flow of value from raw material to finished product.

Before tracking the flow of value, however, managers must, as lean production experts James Womack and Daniel Jones write, "specify value." In lean schools, value is "specified" as test scores. In a lean school, teachers are managers who supervise the flow of value through their students, whose job is to produce test scores as efficiently as possible. Unless they contribute to the production or flow of value, abstract values like emotional and social development, safety, comfort, and joy are all considered waste.

Value added assessments are then used to impose rankings upon teachers. Rankings are another key element of the lean production philosophy. As lean management guru Bob Emiliani puts it, "The final element of ... evolving human resource practice was ... an annual forced ranking of all associates." Forced rankings will certainly sound familiar to anyone who's been following the recent attacks on teachers from New York to California, where politicians and media outlets used test-based teacher rankings to publicly humiliate teachers — even when those rankings were statistically meaningless.

Public humiliation is certainly useful for lean managers who seek to place constant pressure on their employees so that, as Womack and Jones write, they can "do more and more with less and less." The primary goal of forced rankings is, however, to shrink the workforce and see how far remaining workers can be stretched before they crack. Emiliani advises managers to "develop an action plan" for the "bottom ten percent" of workers, and if there's no measurable improvement in performance, "the associate would be subject to involuntary separation." For the best of the workers — more work! As Bill Gates proposed last year in the *Washington Post,* policymakers should "get more students in front of top teachers by identifying the top 25 percent of teachers and asking them to take on four or five more students."

Continuous Improvement?

My former school's quality review lauded, among other things, the school's commitment to "continuous refinements and revisions to curriculum." Like teams, continuous improvement is a key component of lean production — and it too sounds great in theory. Who doesn't want to improve continuously? In lean production, however, the goal isn't to continuously develop workers' skills or even improve the quality of their products. What's continuously improved is the production process itself, and the metric for measuring improvement is efficiency.

Of course, as labor educator Charley Richardson has pointed out, efficiency is not an absolute concept, but is socially defined. Richardson notes, "Coffee breaks, production limits and staffing levels are all designed to improve the production process from a worker perspective and are all inefficiencies from a management perspective." In a lean workplace, continuous improvement means the elimination of whatever makes the work process humane and tolerable in order to increase production numbers.

Ultimately, both the worker and the product are of minimal importance. Perfecting the labor process by maximizing efficiency, regardless of the collateral damage to worker or product, is the goal. In lean schools, teaching, learning, and student growth become secondary.

In 2011, the *New York Times* cited my former school as an example of a troubling new trend: schools with high graduation rates whose students are overwhelmingly unprepared for college. That same year, the City University of New York reported that this school's graduates disproportionately required remedial services in college. While this school failed as an academic institution, it had excelled as a laboratory for lean education, implementing all aspects of business-minded reform as aggressively as possible.

The goal of lean education isn't teaching or learning; it's creating lean workplaces where teachers are stretched to their limits so that students can receive the minimum support necessary to produce satisfactory test scores. It is critical for teachers to see this clearly because lean production is indeed "continuous": in other words, it's insatiable. The harder teachers work to satisfy the demands of lean managers, the harder we will be pushed, until we break down. There is no end to this process.

It is equally critical for parents to understand that their children are being subjected to school reforms that are in fact experiments in educational deprivation. The goal of business-minded reformers is not to create "better" schools for children. It's to create leaner schools for administrators to manage with greater ease. Parents and teachers must fight this process together, or student learning in public schools will continue to suffer.

HaymarketBooks

STANDS WITH THE

CHICAGO TEACHERS UNION

in the fight for

quality, public education,

and workers' rights

In resisting standardized testing, today's teachers are part of a rich tradition of struggle against dehumanization in the workplace.

The Industrial
Classroom

SHAWN GUDE

Michelle Gunderson hates standardized tests. The Chicago elementary school teacher thinks they steal "precious instructional time" and drive a wedge between her and her students.

When Gunderson is forced to administer one of the exams herself, "it is so different from my day-to-day interactions with children that I prepare them for it. I tell them that I have to speak the exact words in the book, and that it won't sound like me. So in a sense, I hate that this test comes between me and the relationships I have with my students."

Educators in Seattle have voiced similar objections. Last January, teachers at Garfield High School announced they would no longer proctor the MAP test, a standardized exam they regard as flawed and detrimental to student learning, and whose implementation was marred by conflict-of-interest concerns.

Jesse Hagopian, a Garfield High history teacher, told me last year that some anti-MAP teachers have a beef only with this particular test; a better one would mollify their misgivings. A large contingent, however, takes issue with standardized tests themselves. "Many others see the problem as more inherent to norm-referenced tests," says Hagopian, referring to exams that place students in "percentiles" and rank them in relation to previous test-takers. "This is a struggle about the MAP test," he says, "but I think the reason why there's been so much support from around the country is it's in the context of a country that's gone test-crazy."

This stance places Hagopian, Gunderson, and other dissident teachers at the center of an upsurge seeking to combat the corporate school-reform movement. They are the counterweights to the well-funded reformers, who push high-stakes testing, competition, and merit pay. They are the bulwarks — the most militant instance being the fall 2012 Chicago Teachers Union strike — against the top-down imposition of policies that drain the profession and the classroom of their humanity.

And in this struggle, the teachers can claim historical antecedents.

A few of their working-class forebears: the Florida educators who launched the first statewide teachers' strike in 1968, seeking increased education funding and signaling an emerging militancy; the pioneering Chicago educators who, tired of crowded classrooms and crappy pay, formed the country's first union composed entirely of teachers; the many workers who, in the early twentieth century, resisted the implementation of so-called "scientific management" in their shops and factories. In each instance, workers fought dehumanization, indignity, and domination. They embodied the labor movement's great promise, that workers acting in concert can control the terms, conditions, and material benefits of their labor.

There's a special resemblance between the struggles against scientific management, or Taylorism, and today's teacher resistance to corporate reform schemes. Just as factory workers fought top-down dictates, deskilling, and the installation of anemic work processes, so

too are teachers trying to prevent the undemocratic implementation of high-stakes testing and merit pay, assaults on professionalism, and the dumbing down and narrowing of curricula.

There are additional parallels: Proponents of scientific management counted some prominent progressives in their ranks, just like the contemporary left-neoliberals hawking education reform. The nostrums of both Taylorism and the education accountability movement paper over foundational conflicts and root causes. Many of those who espouse education reform cast their solutions as unimpeachably "scientific" and "data-driven," yet as with scientific management partisans, the empirical grounding of their prescriptions is highly dubious. And proponents of scientific management and corporate school reform share an antipathy toward unions, often casting them as self-interested inhibitors of progress.

The unions-as-impediment framing is correct in one respect, and here the case of Taylorism is instructive: only organized workers can thwart agents of dehumanization.

———

Born to a wealthy family in 1856, Frederick Taylor was the eponymous champion of the scientific management movement. Less a visionary innovator than a skilled synthesizer, Taylor combined largely preexisting management tools and techniques to develop a coherent system that ratcheted up the amount of control bosses had over workers and the labor process. The stopwatch was his favored metric, the time study his guide. Taylor's objective was to "rationalize" the production process, to expunge it of perceived inefficiencies and increase output. All the waste — gratuitous motions, worker "soldiering," idiosyncratic production methods — had to go.

Non-labor superfluity was included in this, but Taylorism's impact on workers, especially skilled workers, aroused the most opposition. As labor historian David Montgomery details in *Workers' Control in America*, Taylor was confronting craftsmen who had a high degree of autonomy and control over their work. In the late 1800s, skilled workers — even in non-union shops — commonly set an output quota, or "stint," to ensure they'd receive decent pay and regular employment. If managers tried to goad workers into abandoning the collectively set rules, they'd often just walk off the job. They held such power because they alone possessed the "secrets of the craft" — only they knew how to make, mold, and maneuver.

Scientific management's proponents also consciously strove to individualize and atomize workers and break the bonds of solidarity. Increasing and individualizing worker pay served two purposes: inducing otherwise obdurate workers to go along with management's demands, and holding individual workers accountable for their output. In Taylor's eyes, solidarity and collective bargaining were impediments to a genuinely scientific production process. They prevented workers from pursuing their rational self-interest, which, conveniently enough, meant accepting a workplace structured and run according to scientific management's tenets.

Early in his career, as he tried vainly to get individual workers to churn out more than their peers, Taylor conceded that their umbrage was justified. He would act the same way if he were operating the lathe machine. But later, he tended to ascribe a kind of false consciousness to recalcitrant workers. His method was scientific, objective, infallible. What was there to quibble with? Why hadn't the appeal of collective bargaining and unions collapsed under the sheer weight of Taylorism's analytical rigor? Why didn't workers perceive their self-interest?

Louis Brandeis, active in the Progressive Movement and dubbed the "people's lawyer," wondered the same thing. Credulous but avowedly pro-union, he was among the well-intentioned center-left figures who sung the praises of scientific management. Brandeis saw endemic inefficiency in the monopolistic railroads, and, in the widely covered "Eastern Rate Case," introduced an expert who claimed the railroads could save up to $1 million a day. With more money to go around, class antagonism could be ameliorated, if not eradicated. Efficiency would rid the nation of bitter class wars.

Around the same time, scientific management was seeping into the education world. Popular publications like *Ladies' Home Journal* and *Saturday Evening Post*, caught up in the "efficiency craze" and convinced of scientific management's universal applicability, zeroed in on the public education system and shook their heads at the waste and lack of accountability they saw. Unlike scientific management's adherents in private industry, however, they didn't face organized worker opposition. The few existing teachers' unions were young and not major actors. The National Education Association was more a professional organization for administrators than a bona fide union.

Rank-and-file teachers had little role in shaping education policy. Superintendents, as Raymond Callahan chronicles in *Education and the Cult of Efficiency*, were the ones who bore the brunt of the efficiency backlash. And they tended to bend to the critics' wishes. Businesses required a trained workforce, so an "efficient" education system to them meant an increasingly vocationalized one.

———

As a rule, the past few decades have been marked by a pronounced uptick in standardized testing and regimentation. Xian Barrett, who teaches law and Chicago history to high school juniors and seniors, told me that the prioritization of test prep is crowding out more engaging school activities like trips to DC to meet elected officials. The testing obsession, Barrett said, has also increased

the stress level in an already high-stress occupation. "The proliferation of high-stakes testing has … created unnecessary pressure and urgency where those qualities already existed. It has essentially placed a higher burden on those with the toughest jobs — not just the teachers, but other educators and students as well."

Long-time educators like Gunderson, a twenty-seven-year veteran, have seen teachers' control over curriculum threatened and eroded. They've seen the status of their profession diminished. In Chicago specifically, they've seen the predominance of mayoral control — the school board is appointed, not democratically elected — and private largesse in molding public policy. They've watched testing be used to "sort, punish, and privatize," in Gunderson's words. It's put educators on the defensive. "It's not enough to want child-centered learning. You have to be willing to defend it at every turn," the fourth-grade teacher says. "This seems like a silly waste of time and is very different from when I started teaching. I was left alone to make my own sound judgments and was trusted."

The common retort from neoliberal reformers is that teachers must be subject to accountability, and that the most objective way to measure teacher performance is student test scores. Many also favor releasing those figures to the public (so parents can determine the effectiveness of their child's present or future teacher) and linking pay to exam results. But test scores are a notoriously poor way to gauge teacher quality. Student backgrounds, while certainly not determinative, can still impact educational achievement as much as classroom teaching. Equating good teaching with good test scores reduces a complex, human process, and the teacher-student relationship, to a cold data point, bereft of nuance. Under neoliberal reform, rote learning and "teaching to the test" replace critical thinking and problem solving. Taylor's "one best way" is reborn as the "one best answer."

Teachers who balk at high-stakes testing do so because of their love of the profession and support for a lively curriculum, not to inhibit student achievement (or, as Taylor might have framed it, restrict production). Teachers don't "sabotage" their pupils as a defiant worker might a product on an assembly line — the "products" teachers are assembling and molding are living, breathing human beings.

Teachers are, however, fighting incursions on labor autonomy and self-direction that are very reminiscent of Taylorism. As Harry Braverman argues in *Labor and Monopoly Capital*, Taylorism was a program of dehumanization. Properly conceived, human labor is purposeful, deliberately designed, and consciously carried out. The work environment that Taylorists favored — regimented, dictated, with conception divorced from practice — was organized according to the needs of management rather than labor. Workers' wellbeing was an afterthought, entering into the equation only if its consideration could be shown to boost production or prevent labor strife. This amounted to what Braverman calls "the degradation of work," a trend that continued apace through the twentieth century and, to this day, hasn't abated. The same can be said about the corporate school-reform agenda: it results in the "degradation of education."

When education is reduced to test prep, rich curricula and the craft of teaching are imperiled. The vapid classroom of neoliberal school reform mirrors the vapid workplace of Taylorism. Teach for America, which implicitly advances the idea that the sparsely trained can out-teach veteran educators, engenders deskilling and deprofessionalization. Non-practitioners dictating to practitioners how they should do their work mirrors management's disciplining of workers; both militate against work as a creative activity. The appropriation of business language — the head of the Chicago Public Schools is the "CEO" — reinforces the idea that schools should be run like corporations. Merit pay individualizes and severs educators' ties to one another, forcing them to compete instead of cooperate. So too with the anti-union animus that neoliberal reformers and scientific management proponents display.

The goal in each is case to attenuate the collective power of workers to resist management's edicts. The Taylorists' futile efforts to transcend or eradicate class conflict is analogous to corporate school-reformers' sidestepping of child poverty. And prominent Democrats like Barack Obama and his education secretary, Arne Duncan, are school reform's useful idiots, just as prominent Progressive and Taylorist Louis Brandeis was in his day.

This is a simulacrum of schooling. It's education drained of its humanity.

One could easily read the foregoing, nod in agreement, then reasonably object that the analogy between Taylorism and school reform is off in one crucial respect: motivation. Taylor, the skeptic might say, was acting in the service of capital, disciplining labor to increase output. School reformers, however wrongheaded, are legitimately trying to boost student achievement. This argument contains a kernel of truth, and indeed, the private and public spheres are governed by disparate laws and logics. As much as reformers are given to business-speak, public schools still aren't driven entirely by the imperatives of profit, as in the private sector.

For his part, Hagopian sees corporate reform as a deliberate attempt to weaken teachers' unions, one of the few remaining bastions of American labor. "One of the ways to undermine those unions," Hagopian says, "is to make teachers' jobs more tenuous, make people fear for their jobs, and get around union protections by pretending to demand teacher quality and instead implementing these value-added junk-science measures that are not designed to improve student learning."

But one doesn't even have to buy Hagopian's reform-as-subterfuge argument to object to the reform agenda. The motivations of corporate school-reformers are almost immaterial. It's evident that the consequences of the policies they push are injurious to unions. The same can be said about a panoply of reform prescriptions: we needn't speculate about nefarious intent when we know that high-stakes testing narrows curricula and drains the teaching profession of its humanity. We needn't impute bad faith to Wendy Kopp, the founder of Teach for America, when we know her in-and-out-in-two-years model vitiates teaching as a profession. We needn't think that Bill Gates, who single-handedly shapes public education policy, is motivated by malice; simple disgust at its diminution of democracy is enough.

———

So what can reform skeptics learn from the anti-Taylorists of yesteryear?

First, though least auspicious and most obvious: it's an uphill battle. With unemployment low, workers successfully resisted scientific management through World War I, only to have the postwar depression eviscerate unions, wages, and worker power. According to Montgomery, supporters of Taylorism could boast that "the essential elements of their proposals had found favor in almost every industry by the mid 1920s."

Corporate reform appears to be on a similar trajectory. Beaten back in some districts, it nevertheless remains on the march. Charter schools have expanded exponentially over the past decade and now number more than 5,000, operate in more than 40 states, and enroll more than 2 million students. The number of tests given — and the money spent on them — varies by state, but a recent Brookings Institution report estimated that, in total, states shell out about $1.7 billion annually for assessments. And because under capitalism economic power is political power, wealthy philanthropists (see Joanne Barkan's contribution in this booklet) play an outsized role in determining the fate of public education. Top-down decision-making is the order of the day.

Second, union leaders aren't always the friends of rank-and-file members. Samuel Gompers, the conservative president of the American Federation of Labor, initially opposed Taylorism, only to do an about-face and take a collaborationist stance. One could easily tar American Federation of Teachers President Randi Weingarten with the same collaborationist brush. To her credit, Weingarten and the AFT backed the Garfield boycott. Yet she's also shown a penchant for conciliation when confrontation would be the best tactic.

Unionization was a necessary, but insufficient, step in arresting Taylorism's advance. Teachers' unions have played the same role vis-à-vis education reform. But will it be enough? Fortunately, reform skeptics do have a model for resistance: the CTU strike was a "critical example," according to Hagopian. "I think it probably helped our union here see that if you wage a battle, you can win." The union has indeed distinguished itself as neoliberal school-reformers' most

implacable foe. With a new, more militant leadership at the helm, it successfully went on strike — over pay, yes, but also over working conditions, personnel, and resources. Polls showed that parents and community members supported the strikers, in no small part because they spent significant time organizing those groups beforehand and articulated a compelling counter-vision for public education. In Seattle, Garfield High teachers were successful in forcing out the MAP test at the high school level. Unionization in charter schools is slowly increasing. Yet these bright spots are being overshadowed by mass school closings and pronounced privatization in cities like Philadelphia.

The anti-reform fight should not be understood as an anti-progressive, hidebound resistance to inexorable technological and historical advancement. Anti-corporate reform educators aren't hostile to educational progress. They're fighting a neoliberal model in which teachers as agents — subjects teaching subjects — are reduced to objects constrained and acted upon, told what to do and how to do it.

Still, Braverman reminds us that the analogous case of scientific management is a sobering one: "If Taylorism does not exist as a separate school today, that is because, apart from the bad odor of the name, it is no longer the property of a faction, since its fundamental teachings have become the bedrock of all work design." Hopefully, this time around, democracy and humanism will prevail.

Students, particularly those of color, are being pushed out of school and into the criminal legal system. And the corporate reform movement is only making it worse.

Arresting
the Carceral
State

MARIAME KABA & ERICA R. MEINERS

In 2013, the American Civil Liberties Union (ACLU) published a listicle on *Buzzfeed* highlighting the egregious ways young people have been criminalized in American schools. Titled "11 Students Whose Punishments We Wish Were Made Up," examples included "a 12-year-old student in Texas [who] was charged with a misdemeanor for spraying herself with perfume and 'disrupting class.'" In another case a dropped piece of cake in the lunchroom triggered the arrest of a 16-year-old California student who, courtesy of a school police officer, ended up with a broken wrist.

Across the nation eerily similar stories proliferate. Students, particularly those of color, are being pushed out of school and into the criminal legal system through excessive suspensions, expulsions, arrests, and an over-reliance on high stakes testing. Or they are slotted into special education classes — a one-way ticket to an individualized under-education plan.

Increasing numbers of policy makers, advocates, academics, educators, parents, students, and organizers are focusing explicitly on the relationships between education and imprisonment, also known as the school-to-prison pipeline (STPP). Less a pipeline than a nexus or a swamp, the STPP is generally used to refer to interlocking sets of structural and individual relationships in which youth, primarily of color, are funneled from schools and neighborhoods into under- or unemployment and prisons. (The term has its origins in a 2003 gathering.)

While the US public education system has historically diverted non-white communities toward under-education, non-living-wage work, participation in a permanent war economy, and/or incarceration, the development of the world's largest prison nation over the last three decades has strengthened policy, practice, and ideological linkages between schools and prisons. Non-white, non-heterosexual, and/or non-gender conforming students are targeted for surveillance, suspended and expelled at higher rates, and are much more likely to be charged, convicted, and removed from their homes, or otherwise to receive longer sentences.

Criminalizing student behavior is not new. The concept of the "school resource officer" emerged in the 1950s in Flint, Michigan as part of a strategy to embed police officers in community contexts. In 1975, only 1 percent of US schools reported having police officers. As of 2009, New York City schools employed over 5,000 school safety agents and 191 armed police officers, effectively making the school district the fifth largest police district in the country.

This culture of control and surveillance mirrors the intensification of state punishment. Starting in the 1970s — despite a decline in the rates of crime (not always a measure of harm) — states implemented "tough on crime" policies that built the world's largest prison population and did not make communities stronger or safer. A carceral logic, or a punishment mindset, crept into nearly every government function, including those seemingly removed from prisons. Those seeking food stamps are subject to mandatory and/or random drug testing. Immigration and Customs Enforcement has become the

*The story of the Chicago Teachers Strike:
the defining struggle for workers rights
and school reform of our time.*

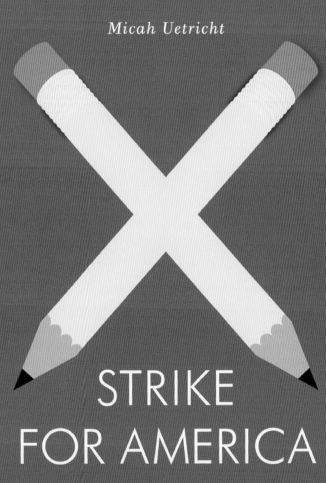

Micah Uetricht

STRIKE
FOR AMERICA

CHICAGO TEACHERS AGAINST AUSTERITY

Available March 2014 / $14.95 PB/Ebook

www.versobooks.com

VERSO

largest enforcement agency in the US. Post-secondary education applications ask about criminal records, and many states bar those with felony convictions from voting.

In k–12 education, high-stakes testing is a proxy for "accountability," and "low-performing" schools are punished with closure while charter schools continue to open. After a few high-profile school shootings in the early 1990s, states introduced "zero tolerance" discipline policies to address a wide range of behaviors schools identified as undesirable. The subsequent increase in surveillance cameras, security guards, metal detectors, and punitive school discipline policies doubled the number of students suspended from school from 1.7 million a year in 1974 to 3.7 million in 2010. The impact of suspensions is clear. Suspended students are three times more likely to drop out by the tenth grade than peers who have never been suspended.

Paralleling our unjust criminal legal system, students of color are, unsurprisingly, targets in schools. One of every four African-American public school students in Illinois was suspended at least once for disciplinary reasons during the 2009–10 school year, the highest rate among the 47 states examined by the Center for Civil Rights Remedies.

While overall youth school-based arrests in Chicago Public Schools (cps) are down from a peak of more than 8,000 in 2003, black youth are still disproportionately arrested. In 2012, black students, who represent about 42 percent of the total cps population, accounted for *75.5 percent of school-based arrests*. Again, mimicking what is happening in the juvenile justice system, the vast majority of these school-based arrests are for misdemeanor offenses (84 percent) as opposed to felonies (16 percent). In other words, youth are not being arrested for serious violent acts or for bringing a weapon to school, but for disrespect or "fighting." Often the term used to describe the differentials between white and black suspension and arrest is "disproportionality," but this term masks the central roles white supremacy and anti-black racism play in shaping ideas and practices surrounding school discipline.

Yet we won't solve the stpp problem by simply changing school disciplinary policies. Because many states spend more on prisons than education, we have to change funding priorities as well. Take Illinois, for example. Between 1985 and 2005, the state built over 25 new prisons or detention facilities. Over the same span, no new public colleges or universities were established. Funding reform

initiatives for K–12 education, mandated by the Illinois State Su-
preme Court, have stalled for decades — ensuring that poor and/or
communities of color still receive significantly less money.

The increased reliance on high-stakes testing also contributes
to the STPP by encouraging a drill-and-test culture within schools
that tends to supplant art, music, and physical education. Many
students, finding the curriculum increasingly irrelevant, disengage
and are subsequently pushed out of school. In a landscape where
market-based reforms have naturalized competition between students and across districts, where failure always results in sanctions,
some struggling schools actively weed out students who do not
meet the requirements of the test. In Florida, for example, schools
have suspended low-performing students in order to improve their
overall test results. Encouragingly, students, teachers, and parents
have protested this practice of teaching to the test, with calls to treat
them as "more than a score."

Additionally, attacks on workplace rights are tied to the carceral logic. Corporate-driven reforms that reshape schools as sites of temporary and unprotected labor constrain school personnel's capacity to interrupt the STPP. We know that students benefit when teachers have workplace protections that foster speech, independent thinking, and advocacy. The push to de-professionalize and de-unionize school personnel — and reframe teachers as Peace Corps lightworkers — transforms teachers into precariously employed charity workers with few rights and meager compensation.

In current circulations of corporate education reform, the image of the lazy, negligent, unionized, female teacher has emerged as a figure to despise. In tandem, the unruly black and brown children require the discipline and order that can only be achieved through schools' intimate partnership with the police, the military, and the business community. This is a recipe for disaster. As the Chicago Teachers Union repeatedly reminded us in their successful fall 2012 strike, teachers' working conditions are students' learning conditions. If educators are forced to teach to tests that don't actually measure student learning, have no employment security but instead are "at will" workers, and are de-professionalized beyond belief, teachers are significantly less likely to support cultures within schools that resist racial profiling or to build other mechanisms to address harm in their schools.

What to do?

We are part of, and committed to, national and local organizing that is building restorative and transformative justice into schools and communities. These philosophies and practices of justice, in contrast to retributive ones, seek to empower communities to respond holistically to violence and harm. Restorative and transformative justice take into account the needs of those affected by an incident of harm, the contexts that produced or shaped harm, and seek to transform or rebuild what was lost rather than view punishment as a final resolution. We desperately need our schools and communities to become restorative and transformative spaces.

We also know the best way to prevent future incarceration is to invest in people and communities and provide excellent educational opportunities for all. A 2007 study estimated that for each potential dropout who completed high school, the US could save $209,000 in prison and other costs. Why not shift budgets from cops in schools to counselors, from building prisons to opening up additional spaces in free public colleges and universities? Instead of more militarized borders, why not ensure that all youth have access to meaningful, discipline-building cocurricular activities such as music, drama, art, and sports?

These are not just pipe dreams. Communities are pushing back and building the world we need. Groups like Chicago's Community Organizing and Family Issues (COFI) have developed downloadable resources for parents on how to advocate for and build restorative justice practices at their children's schools. (As COFI has documented, implementing community peace rooms staffed by parents and volunteers has reduced suspensions and had a positive effect on attendance and behavior.) In the last few years, a network of community groups has emerged offering both spaces to dialogue and concrete ideas on how everyday people can build safety that is not reliant on criminalization — from New York's Audre Lorde Project, to Chicago's Project NIA, to Oakland's Story Telling and Organizing Project.

In addition, teachers are changing classroom practices and school cultures by constructing alternatives. Restorative justice is essentially an unfunded initiative, but teachers across the country are hungry for options. In Chicago over the last couple of years, teachers have crowded workshops at the Teachers for Social Justice Curriculum Fair and other sites to learn how to support this paradigm shift, and how to build alternatives to harsh disciplinary policies.

We participate in, and are excited by, organizing that takes as a starting point the interconnections between struggles to dismantle our carceral state and to build just and flourishing public K–16 educational systems. These include: LGBTQ liberation movements that reject criminalization as the response to gender and sexual violence in schools; immigration rights organizers that say no to legislation that pits children against parents; and anti-violence movements that do not rely on policing as their primary strategy for peace-building. As the black feminist lesbian poet and scholar Audre Lorde wrote years ago, "there are not single issue struggles because we do not live single issue lives."

Arresting the flow of young people from communities into prisons requires rethinking and rebuilding across multiple systems and structures. Schools are just one site for this labor, and we are heartened to see the promising efforts across the country to build them into restorative and transformative spaces.

Education is important, but hardly the answer to inequality.

Unremedial
Education

DEAN BAKER

I t's common in policy circles to claim that improving the quality of education in inner cities and impoverished rural areas is the answer to halting the growing gap between rich and poor. This view reflects not only illusions about the potential for substantially improving education for children from low- and moderate-income families without deeper economic and political shifts, but also a serious misunderstanding about the growth of inequality over the last three decades.

There should be no surprise, then, that the education reform movement has failed in its effort to boost educational outcomes for children from disadvantaged backgrounds.

At this point, education "reform" is hardly new; it is the establishment consensus, having led the national agenda on education for the last quarter century. The extent to which it has produced gains can be debated, but it has, without a doubt, not turned around struggling schools. The children in these schools still perform consistently worse on standardized tests and have much poorer career prospects than children attending wealthy suburban public schools or private ones.

But even if reform had improved education, it is unlikely to have done much about inequality. People with more education have, on average, done better than those with less education, but the growth in inequality over the last three decades has not been mainly a story of the more educated pulling away from the less educated. Rather, it has been a story in which a relatively small group of people (roughly the top one percent) have been able to garner the bulk of economic gains for reasons that have little direct connection to education.

The classic story of the education and inequality story is usually captured by the college/non-college premium: the ratio of the pay of those with college degrees to those without college degrees. This premium showed a substantial rise in the 1980s for both men and women. According to data from the Economic Policy Institute, the college premium for men rose from 20.2 percent at the 1979 business cycle peak to 34 percent at the business cycle peak in 1989. For women, the premium rose from 25 percent in 1979 to 40.0 percent in 1989.

Interestingly, the sharpest rise, especially for men, was during the high unemployment years at the start of the decade. The rise in the college/non-college pay gap is often attributed to technology and the growing use of computers in the workplace, in particular. But the largest rise in the college premium occurred at a point in time when computers were just being introduced to the workplace.

If the timing of the rise in the pay gap in the 1980s doesn't fit the technology story very well, the wage trend in the last two decades is even harder to square with this picture. There was a much smaller increase in the college premium in the 1990s than in the 1980s — even though this was the period of the tech boom, when information technology led to a marked acceleration in the rate of productivity growth. After having risen by almost 14 percentage points in the 1980s business cycle, the college premium for men rose by just 8 percentage points from 1989 to the business cycle peak in 2000. For women, the premium increased by 7.9 percentage points in the 1990s cycle after increasing 15 percentage points in the 1980s.

The 2000s don't fit any better with the technology and inequality story, as even college grads could no longer count on sharing in the gains from growth. For men, the premium rose by 2.8 percentage points between 2000 and 2011. This corresponded to a 2.4 percent gain in wages for male college grads between 2000 and 2012. The college premium for women increased by just 0.8 percentage points over this period, with the wages of female college grads rising by 0.7 percent between 2000 and 2012. This situation holds true even if we look at just the segments of the labor market where we might expect especially strong demand. The average hourly wage for college graduates working in computer and mathematical occupations increased by just 5.3 percent from 2000 to 2011 — less than one-third of the rate of productivity growth over this period.

The patterns in the data show that inequality is not a question of the more-educated gaining at the expense of the less-educated due to inevitable technological trends. Rather, it has been a story in which a small group of especially well-situated workers — for example, those in finance, doctors, and top-level corporate executives — have been able to gain at the expense of almost everyone else. This pattern of inequality will be little affected by improving the educational outcomes for the bottom quarter or even bottom half of income distribution.

Of course, this does not argue against efforts to improve education. It is almost always the case that workers with more education do better than workers with less education, both in terms of hourly wages and employment outcomes. Unemployment and non-employment rates are considerably higher for those with less education.

Education does provide a clear avenue for mobility. Certainly it is a positive development if children from low-income families have the opportunity to move into the middle class, even if this might imply that someone from a middle-class background will move in the opposite direction.

And education is tremendously valuable for reasons unrelated to work and income. Literacy, basic numeracy skills, and critical thinking are an essential part of a fulfilling life. Insofar as we have children going through school without developing these skills, it is an enormous failing of society. Any just society would place a top priority on ensuring that all children learn such basic skills before leaving school.

However, it clearly is not the case that plausible increases in education quality and attainment will have a substantial impact on inequality. This will require much deeper structural changes in the economy. As a practical matter, given the dismal track record of the education reformers, substantial improvement in outcomes for children from low- and moderate-income families is likely to require deep structural change in society as well.

Running
from
Superman

Ignoring — all social and economic factors, corporate reformers shift the burden of failure — onto students.

A Generation at Risk

MEGAN ERICKSON

T he year Ronald Reagan was elected to his first term, the GOP's educational agenda consisted of two main objectives: "bring God back into the classroom" and abolish the Department of Education. This put Reagan's Secretary of Education, Terrel Bell, in an awkward position. Pressured to dismantle the very organization he'd been chosen to oversee, Bell asked the president to devise a national task force on American education, which he hoped would show the necessity of federal involvement in public schools. Bell, notorious within the cabinet for being too liberal, was ignored.

He responded by assembling the task force himself. Chaired by David Pierpont Gardner, president of the University of Utah and an active member of the Church of Latter Day Saints, the eighteen members of the National Commission on Excellence in Education (NCEE) were charged with synthesizing a vast archive of data that had been collected but never before analyzed by the Department of Education and making recommendations based on their findings. In his autobiography, *The Thirteenth Man: A Reagan Cabinet Memoir*, Bell insists that he did not even hint to the NCEE what these recommendations should be — and yet, his designs were evident: "I wanted to stage an event that would jar the people into action on behalf of their educational system," he writes. Milt Goldberg, a prominent member of the commission, later remarked in an interview that he believed Bell had always seen the NCEE "as a way to shore up the Department of Education."

In 1983, the NCEE released *A Nation at Risk: The Imperative for Educational Reform* — arguably the most influential document on education policy since Congress passed Title I in 1965. But where Title I took an *equalizing* approach to reform, prioritizing the distribution of funds to districts comprised primarily of students from low-income families, *A Nation at Risk* called for higher expectations for *all* students, regardless of socioeconomic status: "We must demand the best effort and performance from all students, whether they are gifted or less able, affluent or disadvantaged, whether destined for college, the farm, or industry."

At the time of the report's release, Americans were, as Bell recalls, fraught with anxiety over job loss, inflation, international industrial competition, and a perceived decline in prestige due to the hostage crisis in Iran. Education ranked low on the list of national priorities. So the NCEE used the language of warfare to conflate what was supposedly a crisis in public schools with a crisis in national security. The "risk" in the title refers to the once unthinkable loss of global dominance. The US was threatened by a "rising tide of mediocrity," said the authors of the report, and, somewhat more ambiguously, by a lack of a shared vision. Riding the most recent wave of hysteria over the Cold War, they warned, "If an unfriendly foreign power had attempted to impose on America the mediocre educational performance that exists today, we might well have viewed it as an act of war."

The problem, as they saw it, was that kids were graduating from high school unprepared for success in a global economy. Their solution was more effort, with an emphasis on the advancement of students' personal, educational, and occupational goals. A list of action items to be implemented immediately included: performance-based salaries for teachers, the use of standardized tests for evaluation, grade placement determined by progress rather than by age, the shuttling of disruptive students to alternative schools, increased homework load, attendance policies with incentives and sanctions, and the extension of the school day — in other words, longer, harder hours. Every one of these ideas is rooted in the free market ideology of business. For the first time since Sputnik, the role of the public schools had been reimagined as a kind of baptism by fire into the competitive world of adulthood.

"Overall, I felt that [Reagan] could support its findings and recommendations while rejecting massive federal spending," says Bell. As one journalist noted at the time, the language of *A Nation at Risk* was clearly meant to jar Reagan into action. By that measure, the report was a smashing success. The publicity inspired by the narrative of a hidden crisis in the public schools made it politically impossible for Reagan to shut down the Department of Education. And the incorporation of free market language gave him a reason to embrace it, which he did, a year later — taking credit for having assembled the commission in his 1984 State of the Union Address.

In 1988, Congress's reauthorization of ESEA (the bill that provides federal funding to American public schools) required for the first time that states "define the levels of academic achievement that poor students should attain" and "identify schools in which students were not achieving as expected." George H. W. Bush, Reagan's Republican successor, referred to himself as the "Education President," an issue the Republicans had previously been happy to let the Democrats own. The conventional wisdom that schools were in crisis was now accepted as fact.

But had the NCEE really understood the data they were tasked with analyzing? *A Nation at Risk* contains zero citations, making its claims difficult to verify. Two sociologists of education, David Berliner and Bruce Biddle, have argued that a main point on which the authors based their recommendations — that SAT scores had steadily declined since the 1960s — was actually a misinterpretation of the data. As a voluntary test taken specifically by those intending to go to college, the SAT should never have been aggregated to evaluate the quality of teachers or schools. The slight drop in test scores interpreted by the commission to mean that America's schools (and its prosperity, security, and civility) were spiraling downward, instead reflected a postwar shift toward inclusion, as more and more people signed up to take the test. Disaggregated data shows that math scores for all groups during the years preceding the release of the report increased, while verbal scores remained constant.

A Nation at Risk also failed to recognize that achievement in the more affluent districts of the US is relatively strong compared to students in other countries. US test scores are lower than those of Canada and Sweden because we have a disproportionate amount of low-income students compared to those countries (over 20% of children in the United States live in poverty). One of the few consistent findings of education researchers is that concentrated poverty lowers the quality of education in every school where the percentage of poor students rises above a certain level. Class integration, it seems, is the only proven means of raising educational outcomes.

The American habit of viewing public schools as the great equalizer of our society has often lead us to graft our fantasies, anxieties, and dreams onto the education system. For most of our history, education has been the only real form of a social safety net, meaning that the schools are the arena in which social apprehensions are played out. It makes sense then, that as mainstream attitudes toward the problems of the country's growing lower class changed in the 1980s, the way politicians and policymakers talked about the problems facing the nation's schools also changed. If self-reliance was all that was required to compete financially, it followed that raising standards and holding students, parents, and schools accountable was all that was required to succeed academically.

Over the past thirty years, as the focus of educational policy has shifted from equity to excellence, the gaps in achievement between black and white students and rich and poor students have widened. The gains of the 1970s are gone. "Excellence" and equity have been shown to be almost mutually exclusive in practice.

Of course, *A Nation at Risk* wasn't influential because it was accurate. It was influential because it was the version of events that American voters and policymakers wanted to believe at the time. It had the convenient effect of converting what had been a material crisis into a struggle for the soul of American schools, a corporeal problem into a deficiency of gumption. Its tantalizingly simplistic implication was that social problems arise not from a specific set of policies and realities — segregation, discrimination, poverty — but from a lack of willpower: the obscure malaise hinted at in *A Nation At Risk*. If a poor kid couldn't succeed, she just didn't have the right attitude. That is not an overstatement; it is the central assumption that animates every initiative we gather together and call education reform.

And though today this view usually hides behind the kind of technocratic utopianism we associate with the Bill & Melinda Gates Foundation, Newt Gingrich's recent comments about what to do with "a school that is failing with a teacher that is failing" cut to the vulgar core of the whole enterprise. Gingrich believes that such schools "ought to get rid of the unionized janitors … and pay local students to take care of the school. The kids would actually do work, they would have cash … they'd begin the process of rising." This may sound crass, but it shouldn't be surprising. It is simply a tactless articulation of the market-based mindset — advocating for choice, merit pay, and standardization of assessments and curriculum — that has dominated policy discussions since the 1980s.

The problem, according to Gingrich, is that poor kids just aren't up to the boot-strapping required for success in today's economy: "Really poor children, in really poor neighborhoods have no habits of working and have nobody around them who works so they have no habit of showing up on Monday." The problem, according to proponents of marketization and accountability, is that poor kids don't have access to the kinds of opportunities — or the system of goals, rewards, and punishments — that would allow them to pull themselves up. The diagnosis is the same: better yourself, work harder, perhaps find a rich mentor, and you will be rewarded. Days after Gingrich was excoriated in the *New York Times*, a blogger at the pro-charter Hoover Institute asked, *Is it time for education reformers to pay Gingrich some more attention?* Yeah, Newt's a goofball, and an easy target for bleeding-heart liberals, the writer argued, but he's also right.

Under the influence of these reformers, the American education system has become less about curriculum and critical thinking, and more like *Oprah*: a program of self-mastery framed as a moral imperative. In public schools across the country, particularly urban ones, social studies and music classes are commonly replaced by the kind of glorified vocational training called for in *A Nation at*

Risk. The pro-charter Gates Foundation, which has spent $5 billion on urban education initiatives over the past ten years, began to advocate that summer internships be made a permanent part of the high school curriculum in 2006. Andrew Carnegie was content to control the building and naming of cultural institutions; the new wave of philanthrocapitalists, with Gates at the forefront, wants a say in what goes on inside them.

With donor cash comes a set of beliefs, awkwardly transplanted from the business world to the classroom: the management guru's vision of empowerment as a personal struggle, the CEO's conviction that individual success is limited only by a lack of ambition, life as a series of goals waiting to be met. The type of advice once reserved for dieters, rookie sales associates, and the unemployed is now repeated to public school children with new age fervor: *Think positive. Set goals and achieve them. Reach for the stars. Race to the top. It's never too early to network. Just smile.* Like the promise of *A Nation at Risk*, these admonitions are at once wildly idealistic and bitterly cruel: "You forfeit your chance for life at its fullest when you withhold your best effort in learning.... When you work to your full capacity, you can hope to attain the knowledge and skills that will enable you to create your future and control your destiny. If you do

not, you will have your future thrust upon you by others." Convert every challenge into an opportunity, or else.

But who will coach you towards your goals? As it happens, this is exactly the kind of thing at which the business community excels. A new genre of nonprofits has been invented solely for the purpose of connecting business leaders with high school principals. The website for PENCIL, one such organization, features pictures of prominent business people (the VP of human capital management at Goldman Sachs, the CEO of JetBlue) smiling in front of a chalkboard, surrounded by drawings of mountains and spaceships. "See how an airline mogul is encouraging students at Aviation High School to soar. See how a visionary is helping students at P. S. 86K build a greener planet," reads the accompanying text. The business leader is the ultimate embodiment of success. When you conceive of the schools as a holding pen for grooming tomorrow's talent, it makes sense to turn to him or her for expert counsel. This is exactly the kind of thinking that led New York City Schools Chancellor Dennis Walcott to plea to the business community for support on PENCIL's behalf. The message to businesses: we need you now more than ever.

Just as Oprah's exhortation to Live Your Best Life was eventually stamped and sold on a line of low-calorie packaged foods, a for-profit testing industry has risen to provide the instruments of American students' transformation into fearless, proficient, and likable employees. However, neither the food sales, nor the Scantron tests, are the point. The most radical change currently underway in American public schools is the reconceptualization of the role of the student from learner to beneficiary.

A press release for the Goldman Sachs Foundation's Next Generation Fund refers paternalistically to "disadvantaged youth" as "undeveloped 'diamonds in the rough,' unprepared for the intense competition for coveted places in higher education and the professional world." But, as John Dewey wrote, perhaps too optimistically, "Education is not preparation for life; education is life itself." Children are by definition low performers compared to adults. The business leader and the education reformer seek to improve the child, because childhood, in the logic of capitalism, is a temporary setback from productivity which must be overcome. There are two conditions that students and teachers can feel in response: self-mastery or gratitude.

The movement towards higher standards and market-based reforms ignited by *A Nation at Risk* took place within the historical context of an intensifying stratification of resources along race and class lines, and the division of people into leaders and subordinates is an intrinsic aspect of education reform. Its leaders are overwhelmingly adult administrators, philanthropists, and venture capitalists (usually men) while the people who are most affected by it are teachers (usually women) and children with comparatively little or no economic power. The crisis we face is one of inequality and wealth distribution, not a vague collective decline towards sloppiness.

It is questionable whether public schools have actually "failed" on a national level, but even if that's the case, the failure is systemic, not the product of the inexplicable, synchronized mediocrity of a few individuals who need a little encouragement. The religion of self-improvement is a way of redirecting criticisms or outrage from socio-economic structures back to the individual, imprisoning any reformist or revolutionary impulse within our own feelings of inadequacy — which is why the process of improving our nation's schools has taken on the tone of a spiritual cleansing rather than a political reckoning. Now, instead of saying "our socioeconomic system is failing us," an entire generation of children will learn to say, "I have failed myself."

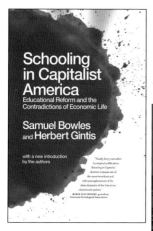

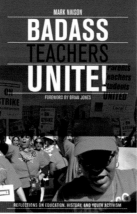

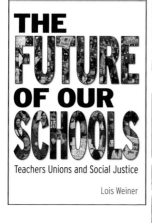

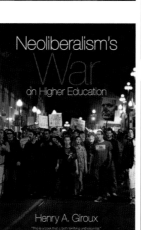

HaymarketBooks
haymarketbooks.org

Teach for America weakens teachers' unions, while doing little to improve students' education.

Education Reform's Trojan Horse

ANDREW HARTMAN

T he history of Teach For America reveals the ironies of contemporary education reform. In its mission to deliver justice to underprivileged children, TFA and the education reform movement have advanced an agenda that aids conservative attempts to undercut teachers' unions. More broadly, TFA has been in the vanguard in forming a neoliberal consensus about the role of public education — and the role of public school teachers — in a deeply unequal society.

In 1988, Princeton student Wendy Kopp wrote a thesis arguing for a national teacher corps modeled on the Peace Corps that "would mobilize some of the most passionate, dedicated members of my generation to change the fact that where a child is born in the United States largely determines his or her chances in life." Kopp launched TFA in 1990 as a not-for-profit charged with selecting the brightest, most idealistic recent college graduates as corps members who would commit to teach for two years in some of the nation's toughest schools.

From its inception, the media anointed TFA the savior of American education. Prior to a single corps member stepping foot in a classroom, the *New York Times* and *Newsweek* lavished Kopp's new organization with cover stories full of praise. Adulation has remained the norm. Its recent twenty-year anniversary summit, held in Washington, DC, featured fawning video remarks by President Obama and a glitzy "who's who" roster of elite cheerleaders, including John Lewis, Malcolm Gladwell, Gloria Steinem, and TFA board member John Legend. The organs of middlebrow centrist opinion — *Time Magazine*, *Atlantic Monthly*, the *New Republic* — glorify TFA at every opportunity. The *Washington Post* heralds the nation's education reform movement as the "TFA insurgency" — a perplexing linguistic choice given so-called "insurgency" methods have informed national education policies from Reagan to Obama.

TFA is, at best, another chimerical attempt in a long history of chimerical attempts to sell educational reform as a solution to class inequality. At worst, it's a Trojan horse for all that is unseemly about the contemporary education reform movement.

The original TFA mission was based on a set of four somewhat noble if paternalistic rationales. First, by bringing the elite into the teaching profession, even if temporarily, TFA would burnish it with a much-needed "aura of status and selectivity." Second, by supplying its recruits to impoverished school districts, both urban and rural, TFA would compensate for the lack of quality teachers willing to work in such challenging settings. And third, although Kopp recognized that most corps members would not remain classroom teachers beyond their two-year commitments, she believed that TFA alums would form the nucleus of a new movement of educational leaders — that their transformative experiences teaching poor children would mold their ambitious career trajectories. Above these three foundational principles loomed a fourth: the mission to relegate educational inequality to the ash heap of history.

TFA goals derive, in theory, from laudable — if misguided — impulses. But each, in practice, has demonstrated to be deeply problematic. TFA underwrites, intentionally or not, the conservative assumptions of the education reform movement: that teachers' unions serve as barriers to quality education; that testing is the best way to assess quality education; that educating poor children is best done by institutionalizing them; that meritocracy is an end-in-itself; that social class is an unimportant variable in education reform; that education policy is best made by evading politics proper; and that faith in public school teachers is misplaced.

Take the first rationale: that TFA would enhance the image of the teaching profession. On the contrary, the only brand TFA endows with an "aura of status and selectivity" is its own. As reported in the *New York Times*, 18 percent of Harvard seniors applied to TFA in 2010, a rate only surpassed by the 22 percent of Yale seniors who sought to join the national teacher corps that year. All told, TFA selected 4,500 lucky recruits from a pool of 46,359 applicants in 2010. Although many applicants are no doubt motivated to join out of altruism, the two-year TFA experience has become a highly desirable notch on the resumes of the nation's most diligent strivers.

The more exclusive TFA becomes, the more ordinary regular teachers seem. TFA corps members typically come from prestigious institutions of higher education, while most regular teachers are trained at the second- and third-tier state universities that house the nation's largest colleges of education. Whereas TFA corps members leverage the elite TFA brand to launch careers in law or finance — or, if they remain in education, to bypass the typical career path on their way to principalships and other positions of leadership — most regular teachers must plod along, negotiating their way through traditional career ladders.

The second justification for TFA — that it exists to supply good teachers to schools where few venture to work — has also proven questionable. Though the assertion made some sense in 1990, when many impoverished school districts did in fact suffer from a dearth of teachers, the same is not so easily argued now. Following the economic collapse of 2008, which contributed to school revenue problems nationwide, massive teacher layoffs became the new norm, including in districts where teacher shortages had provided an entry to TFA in the past. Thousands of Chicago teachers, for instance, have felt the sting of layoffs and furloughs in the past two years, even as the massive Chicago Public School system, bound by contract, continues to annually hire a specified number of TFA corps members. In the face of these altered conditions, the TFA public relations machine now deemphasizes teacher shortages and instead accentuates one crucial adjective: "quality." In other words, schools in poor urban and rural areas of the country might not suffer from a shortage of teachers in general, but they lack for the *quality* teachers that Kopp's organization provides.

After twenty years of sending academically gifted but untrained college graduates into the nation's toughest schools, the evidence regarding TFA corps member effectiveness is in, and it is decidedly mixed. Professors of education Julian Vasquez Heilig and Su Jin Jez, in the most thorough survey of such research yet, found that TFA corps members tend to perform equal to teachers in similar situations — that is, they do as well as new teachers lacking formal training assigned to impoverished schools. Sometimes they do better, particularly in math instruction. Yet "the students of novice TFA teachers perform significantly less well," Vasquez Heilig and Jin Jez discovered, "than those of credentialed beginning teachers." It seems clear that TFA's vaunted thirty-day summer institute — TFA "boot camp" — is no replacement for the preparation given future teachers at traditional colleges of education.

Putting TFA forward to solve the problems of the teaching profession has turned out poorly. But the third premise for Kopp's national teacher corps — that it would "create a leadership force for long-term change" in how the nation's least privileged students are schooled — has been the most destructive. Such destructiveness is directly related to Kopp's success in attaching TFA to the education reform movement. In this, Kopp's timing could not have been more fortuitous. When TFA was founded, the education reform movement was beginning to make serious headway in policy-making circles.

One of the more salient aspects of the so-called "TFA insurgency" was that it operated from the assumption that more resources were not a prerequisite for improving schools. "Schools that transform their students' trajectories aspire not to equality of inputs," Kopp declared, "but rather to equality of outputs." Instead of more resources, underprivileged students needed better teachers. Reformers thus set out to devise a system that hired and retained effective teachers while also driving ineffective ones from the classroom.

The TFA network has been crucial in shaping efforts to improve the nation's teacher force. Kopp's second book, *A Chance to Make History* (2011), reads like a primer for such reform measures. Kopp is particularly enamored by high-performing charter schools, which succeed because they do whatever it takes to hire and retain good teachers, a zero-sum game that most schools cannot win without more resources — those dreaded "inputs." But successful charter schools, Kopp maintains, also stop at nothing to remove bad teachers from the classroom. This is why charter schools are the preferred mechanism for delivery of education reform: as defined by Kopp, charter schools are "public schools empowered with flexibility over decision making in exchange for accountability for results."

And yet, "results," or rather, academic improvement, act more like a fig leaf, especially in light of numerous recent studies that show charter schools tend to do no better, and often do worse, than traditional public schools at educating students. Rather, crushing teachers' unions — the real meaning behind Kopp's "flexibility" euphemism — has become the ultimate end of the education reform movement. This cannot be emphasized enough: the precipitous growth of charter schools and the TFA insurgency are part and parcel precisely because both cohere with the larger push to marginalize teachers' unions.

The TFA insurgency has, from its inception, sold education reform as above politics. The idea is to support ideas that work, plain and simple, no matter their source. But the biography of Michelle Rhee, the prototypical TFA corps member-turned-reformer and the most divisive person in the education reform movement, defies such anti-political posturing. After serving a two-year stint in the Baltimore Public Schools as one of the earliest TFA corps members, she earned a Master's Degree from the Harvard University Kennedy School of Government. From there Kopp tapped Rhee to be the founding CEO of The New Teacher Project, a TFA spin-off that sought to revolutionize the teacher accreditation process by helping school districts evade colleges of education. The notoriety she gained in her work with The New Teacher Project enabled her appointment as Chancellor of Schools in Washington, DC.

Rhee is adored in elite circles. Regularly feted by Oprah, Kopp touts her as a "transformational leader." During her short tenure leading the infamously bad DC schools, Rhee gained national acclaim for applying, in Kopp's admiring words, the corporate "principles of management and accountability."

In contrast to such devotion, teachers' unions loathe Rhee. Rhee's heavy-handedness in dealing with the Washington Teachers' Union conveyed her attitude that a non-unionized teacher force would better serve justice for children, as if children would benefit from their teachers lacking the few remaining benefits accrued by collective bargaining, such as nominal job security and shrinking pensions. Rhee is also disliked by a large percentage of black DC citizens, who voted out former Mayor Adrian Fenty in part because of his unqualified support for Rhee's actions. This included firing 4 percent of district teachers, mostly black, and replacing them largely with TFA-style teachers, mostly white, whom one astute black Washingtonian labeled "cultural tourists."

TFA's complicity in education reform insanity does not stop there. From its origins, the TFA-led movement to improve the teacher force has aligned itself with efforts to expand the role of high-stakes standardized testing in education. TFA insurgents, including Kopp and Rhee, maintain that, even if imperfect, standardized tests are the best means by which to quantify accountability. Prior to the enactment of Bush's bipartisan No Child Left Behind in 2001, high-stakes standardized testing was mostly limited to college-entrance exams such as the Scholastic Aptitude Test (SAT). But since then, the high-stakes testing movement has blown up: with increasing frequency, student scores on standardized exams are tied to teacher, school, and district evaluations, upon which rewards and punishments are meted out.

Obama's "Race to the Top" policy — the brainchild of Secretary of Education Arne Duncan, the former "CEO" of Chicago Public Schools — further codifies high-stakes testing by allocating scarce federal resources to states that most aggressively implement these so-called accountability measures. The multibillion dollar testing industry — dominated by a few large corporations that specialize in the making and scoring of standardized tests — has become an entrenched interest, a powerful component of a growing education-industrial complex.

TFA insurgents support standardized testing not only because they believe it ensures accountability. They also herald testing because it provides evidence that their efforts are working. The schools and districts that achieved celebrity as the reform movement's success stories did so by vastly improving standardized test scores. In emphasizing testing, though, reformers tend to overlook the obvious incentives that ambitious educators have to manipulate statistics. President Bush appointed Houston Superintendent of Schools Rod Paige as Secretary of Education in 2001 because Paige's reform measures seemingly led to skyrocketing graduation rates. Not surprisingly, this so-called "Texas miracle," predicated on falsified numbers, was too good to be true.

More recently, cheating scandals have likewise discredited several celebrated reform projects. In Atlanta, a TFA hotbed, former superintendent and education reform darling Beverly Hall is implicated in a cheating scandal of unparalleled proportions, involving dozens of Atlanta principals and hundreds of teachers, including TFA corps members. Cheating was so brazen in Atlanta that principals hosted pizza parties where teachers and administrators systematically corrected student exams.

Following a series of investigative reports in *USA Today*, a new cheating scandal seems to break every week. Cheating has now been confirmed not only in Atlanta, but also in New York City, Philadelphia, Baltimore, Chicago, Los Angeles, San Francisco, Orlando, Dallas, Houston, Dayton, and Memphis, education reform cities all. Rhee's DC "miracle" has also been clouded by suspicion: impossibly high wrong-to-right erasure rates indicate that several of Rhee's "blue ribbon" schools might have cheated their way to higher test scores. Such accusations are nothing new to Rhee. The legend of how she transformed her Baltimore students — a fable resembling the Hollywood drama *Stand and Deliver*, based on East Los Angeles math teacher Jaime Escalante's work in helping several of his underprivileged students pass the Advanced Placement Calculus exam — has been called into question by investigative reports that suggest fraud.

That education reformers have long argued that "incentives" are necessary to improve the teach-

ing profession underscores another in a series of ironies that mark the movement. Reformers believe that if teachers are subjected to "market forces," such as merit pay and job insecurity, they will work harder to improve the education they provide for their students. The need to incentivize the teaching profession is the most popular argument against teacher's unions, since unions supposedly protect bad teachers. But, in a predictable paradox, by attaching their incentives agenda to standardized testing, the reform movement has induced cheating on a never-before-seen scale, proving the maxim known as Campbell's Law: "The more any quantitative social indicator is used for social decision-making, the more subject it will be to corruption pressures and the more apt it will be to distort and corrupt the social processes it is intended to monitor." In sum, the TFA insurgency's singular success has been to empower those best at gaming the system.

In contrast to such "success," the TFA insurgency has failed to dent educational inequality. This comes as no surprise to anyone with the faintest grasp of the tight correlation between economic and educational inequality: TFA does nothing to address the former while spinning its wheels on the latter. In her writings, nowhere does Kopp reflect upon the patent ridiculousness of her expectation that loads of cash donated by corporations that exploit inequalities across the world — such as Union Carbide and Mobil, two of TFA's earliest contributors — will help her solve some of the gravest injustices endemic to American society. Kopp shows some awareness of the absurdities of her own experiences — including a "fundraising schedule [that] shuttled me between two strikingly different economic spheres: our undersourced classrooms and the plush world of American philanthropy" — but she fails to grasp that this very gap is what makes her stated goal of equality unachievable.

In short, Kopp, like education reformers more generally, is an innocent when it comes to political economy. She spouts platitudes about justice for American children, but rarely pauses to ask whether rapidly growing inequality might be a barrier to such justice. She celebrates twenty years of reform movement success, but never tempers such self-congratulatory narcissism with unpleasant questions about why those who have no interest in disrupting the American class structure — such as Bill Gates and the heirs to Sam Walton's fortunes, by far the most generous education reform philanthropists — are so keen to support the TFA insurgency.

In working to perfect their approach to education, TFA insurgents miss the forest for the trees. They fail to ask big-picture questions. Will their pedagogy of surveillance make for a more humane society? Having spent their formative years in a classroom learning test-taking skills, will their students become good people? Will they know more history? Will they be more empathetic? Will they be better citizens? Will they be more inclined to challenge the meritocracy? Or, as its newest converts, will they be its most fervent disciples? What does it mean that for children born in the Bronx to go to college they must give up their childhoods, however bleak?

In a democracy, educators, parents, children, and voters should determine the direction of public schools — not well-heeled donors.

How Mega-Foundations Threaten Public Education

JOANNE BARKAN

F or a dozen years, huge private foundations have been funding a massive crusade to remake public education for low-income and minority children in the image of the private sector. If schools were run like businesses competing in the market — so the argument goes — the achievement gap that separates poor and minority students from middle-class and affluent students would disappear. The Bill and

Melinda Gates Foundation, the Eli and Edythe Broad Foundation, and the Walton Family Foundation have taken the lead, but other mega-foundations have joined in to underwrite the self-proclaimed "education reform movement." Some of them are the Laura and John Arnold, Anschutz, Annie E. Casey, Michael and Susan Dell, William and Flora Hewlett, and Joyce foundations.

Each year mega-foundations channel about $1 billion to "ed reform." This might look like a drop in the bucket compared to the $525 billion or so that taxpayers spend on K–12 education annually. But discretionary spending — spending beyond what covers ordinary running costs — is where policy is shaped and changed. The mega-foundations use their grants as leverage: they give money to grantees who agree to adopt the foundations' pet policies. Resource-starved states and school districts feel compelled to say yes to millions of dollars even when many strings are attached or they consider the policies unwise. They are often in desperate straits.

Most critiques of the mega-foundations' current role in public education focus on the poor quality of the reforms and their negative effects on schooling — on who controls schools, how classroom time is spent, how learning is measured, and how teachers and principals are evaluated. The harsh criticism is justified. But to examine the effect of the foundations' ed-reform work on democracy and civil society requires a different focus.

Have the voices of "stakeholders" — students, their parents and families, educators, and citizens who support public education — been strengthened or weakened? Has their involvement in public decision-making increased or decreased? Has their grassroots activity been encouraged or stifled? Are politicians more or less responsive to them? Is the press more or less free to inform them? According to these measures, the mega-foundations' involvement has undoubtedly undermined both democracy and civil society.

You Can't Fool All of the People All of the Time

The combination of aggressive style, controversial programs, and abundant money has led some mega-foundations into the world of "astroturfing." This is political activity designed to appear unsolicited and rooted in a local community without actually being so. Well-financed astroturfing suffocates authentic grassroots activity by defining an issue and occupying the space for organizing. In addition, when astroturfers confront grassroots opposition, the astroturfers have an overwhelming advantage because of their resources. Sometimes, however, a backlash flares up when community members realize that paid outsiders are behind a supposedly local campaign.

In 2009, for example, the Gates Foundation funded the creation of a nonprofit organization to stir up grassroots support for the foundation's teacher effectiveness reforms. The reforms used students' scores on standardized tests to evaluate teachers and award bonuses, abolished tenure, and ended seniority as a criterion for salary increases, layoffs, and transfers. Gates paid a philanthropy service group called Rockefeller Philanthropy Advisors (RPA) $3.5 million to set up the new nonprofit. Its staff would target four "sites" — Pittsburgh, Memphis, Hillsborough County (Tampa, Florida), and a consortium of Los Angeles charter schools — where Gates was about to invest $335 million to try out its reforms.

Renamed Communities for Teaching Excellence, the nonprofit was launched in 2010. It survived for barely two years. Operating out of Los Angeles while trying to produce local enthusiasm for controversial policies in Pittsburgh, Memphis, and Tampa didn't work. In addition, there was growing competition: various philanthropies, including Gates, began funding other nonprofits that sent paid staff around the country to start a variety of education reform campaigns. These efforts were also astroturfing, but many had greater success — in part because they had multiple and less identifiable funders. Amy Wilkins, chair of the nonprofit's board of directors, summed up the problem for the *Los Angeles Times* (October 19, 2012): "You have to show broad public support so you're not seen as a phony-baloney front for Gates."

The Parent Trigger Trap

In January 2010 California enacted the nation's first "parent trigger" law. The law gives parents control over the fate of their children's public school if it persistently underperforms — or if they can be persuaded that it underperforms. When the parents (or guardians) of at least half of a school's students sign a trigger petition, the signers can then choose to have the school principal replaced, the entire staff replaced, the school replaced with a privately operated charter, or the school shut down. The law was immediately controversial. The process was bound to divide communities, and it was open to abuse and outside manipulation. But most important, the law destroyed the democratic nature of public education. This year's parents don't have the right to close down a public school or give it away to a private company any more than this year's users of a public park can decide to pave it over or name a private company to run it with tax dollars. Voters — directly or through their elected officials — decide on and pay for public institutions in a democracy.

The mega-foundations' role in the trigger law began with Green Dot, a charter school company with funding from Gates, Broad, Walton, Annenberg, Wasserman, and other foundations. Green Dot created an organization called Parent Revolution to lobby for and then use the law. The Broad Foundation was one of Parent Revolution's first financial backers in 2009. Once the law passed, other foundations jumped in. Parent Revolution now operates nationally and has received more than $14.8 million, most of it from mega-foundations. Walton has given $6.3 million (43 percent of the total). Other major funders are Gates ($1.6 million), Arnold ($1.5 million), Wasserman ($1.5 million), Broad ($1.45 million), and Emerson ($1.2 million).

Parent Revolution didn't wait for actual parents to initiate the trigger process; it hired canvassers to find a serviceable school. The choice was McKinley Elementary in Compton, a city of about 97,000 (97 percent African American and Latino) in Los Angeles County. Parent Revolution drafted the petition, which specified that a charter company called Celerity Education Group would take over McKinley. Paid canvassers, along with fifteen recruited parents, collected signatures and submitted the petition to district headquarters in December 2010. Then the conflict erupted. Some signers maintained they hadn't realized they were choosing the charter school option. Fifty or sixty parents rescinded their signatures. Other parents and the district claimed the petition was invalid because Parent Revolution had imposed not only the charter option, but a specific company. Each side accused the other of harassment, including threatening undocumented residents with deportation. After a court ruled that the petition was invalid, the parent trigger drive at McKinley ended, leaving community members divided and bitter.

Parent Revolution's second effort — at Desert Trails Elementary School in Adelanto, 85 miles northeast of Los Angeles — was equally disruptive. The town of more than 32,000 is about 78 percent Latino and African American. One in three residents lives below the

poverty line; the largest employer is the Adelanto school district. In 2011 Parent Revolution hired a full-time organizer, rented a house for a campaign headquarters, and, according to Gary Cohn (www.fryingpannews.org, 2 April 2013), "sent in experts to train and advise parents on everything from strategy on dealing with the school board to writing letters to help in researching potential charter schools…. It even provided [campaign logo] T-shirts."

After a contentious process, 100 of the 466 parents who had signed the petition for a charter takeover changed their minds and rescinded their signatures. The school board invalidated another 200 signatures. With just 37 percent of parents remaining, the board voted unanimously in March 2012 to reject the petition. Parent Revolution then paid to challenge the board in court. In July a superior court judge ruled that the trigger law did not provide for parents to rescind their signatures.

When petition signers gathered in mid-October 2012 to vote on which charter company would take over the school, only 53 of them showed up. Two parents who opposed Parent Revolution told Cohn why they felt aggrieved. Lori Yuan, mother of two students, said, "We've known all along this wasn't a grassroots movement." Shelly Whitfield, mother of five students, said, "They're taking away all the teachers my kids have been around for years. They took over our school, and I don't think it's fair."

The Very Model of a Modern Major Trigger Law

According to a report by the National Conference of State Legislatures, parent trigger legislation had been brought up in at least twenty-five states as of March 2013. In addition to California, six states have enacted versions of it: Connecticut, Indiana, Louisiana, Mississippi, Ohio (a pilot program in Columbus), and Texas. Much credit for this rapid expansion goes to the American Legislative Exchange Council (ALEC), the now notorious organization of businesses, private foundations, and over 2,000 conservative state legislators. ALEC meets twice a year in closed sessions to draft model legislation on various issues; state representatives can then introduce the bills in their legislatures. According to ALEC's website, "Each year, close to 1,000 bills, based at least in part on ALEC Model Legislation, are introduced in the states. Of these, an average of 20 percent become law." Many of the controversial "stand your ground" self-defense laws, voter ID laws that suppress minority voting, and parent trigger laws are based on ALEC models.

Despite its obviously political agenda, ALEC is a tax-exempt nonprofit. The Gates Foundation gave the group a $376,635 grant in 2011 "to educate and engage its members on efficient state budget approaches to drive greater student outcomes, as well as educate them on beneficial ways to recruit, retain, evaluate and compensate effective teaching based upon merit and achievement." After several exposés of ALEC's work prompted some corporate members to resign, the Gates Foundation announced in 2012 that it would finish out its grant to ALEC but not undertake future funding.

He Who Pays the Piper Calls the Tune

Philanthropies risk losing their tax-exempt status if they donate directly to candidates for public office, so some foundations have tried other ways to ensure they have the people they want in key posts.

The Los Angeles–based Broad Foundation stipulated in the contract for a $430,000 grant to New Jersey's Board of Education that Governor Chris Christie remain in office. As the *Star-Ledger* reported (12 December 2012), the Newark-based Education Law Center had forced the release of the contract through the state's Open Public Records Act. For the center's executive director, David Sciarra, "It is a foundation driving public educational policy that should be set by the Legislature." The Broad Foundation's senior communications director responded, "[W]e consider the presence of strong leaders to be important when we hand over our dollars."

The keep-Chris-Christie clause was not the first time a staffing prerequisite was discovered in a grant contract with a public entity. In 2010 then-Washington, DC schools chancellor Michelle Rhee negotiated promises for $64.5 million in grants from the Broad,

Walton, Robertson, and Arnold foundations. Rhee planned to use part of the money to finance a proposed five-year, 21.6 percent increase in teachers' base salary. In exchange she demanded that the union give her more control over evaluating and firing teachers and allow bonus pay for teachers who raised student test scores. In March 2010 the foundations sent separate letters to Rhee stating that they reserved the right to withdraw their money if she left. They also required that the teachers ratify the proposed contract. Critics challenged not only the heavy-handed intrusion into an acrimonious contract negotiation but also the legality of the stipulation on Rhee: hadn't she negotiated a grant deal that served her own employment interests? The teachers ratified the contract, but the extremely unpopular Rhee resigned in October 2010 after Mayor Adrian Fenty, who had hired her, lost the Democratic mayoral primary. By that time, much of the grant money had been spent, and the new schools chancellor kept Rhee's policies.

Private foundations have used another tactic to exert influence on the Los Angeles Unified School District: they paid the salaries of more than a dozen senior staffers. According to the *Los Angeles Times* (16 December 2009), the privately financed "public" employees worked on such education reform projects as new systems to evaluate teachers and collect immense amounts of data on students. Much of the money came from the Wasserman Foundation ($4.4 million) and the Walton Family Foundation ($1.2 million); Ford and Hewlett made smaller grants. The Broad Foundation covered the $160,000 salary of Matt Hill to run the district's Public School Choice program, which turned so-called low-performing and new schools over to private operators. Hill had worked in Black & Decker's business development group before he went through one of the Broad Foundation's uncertified programs to train new education administrators. As a *Los Angeles Times* editorial (12 January 2010) sensibly asked, "At what point do financial gifts begin reshaping public decision-making to fit a private agenda?... Even the best-intentioned gifts have a way of shifting behavior. Educators and the public, not individual philanthropists, should set the agenda for schools."

Indeed, in a democracy, educators, parents, children, and voters should shape public education — not private mega-foundations.

Manufactured budget crises are being used as a pretext to privatize, close schools, and lay off educators.

Disaster Capitalism, Chicago-style

KENZO SHIBATA

I n public policy circles, crises are called "focusing events" — bringing to light a particular failing in government policy. They require government agencies to switch rapidly into crisis mode to implement solutions. Creating the crisis itself is more novel.

The right-wing, free market vision of University of Chicago economist Milton Friedman informed the blueprint for the rapid privatization of municipal services throughout the world due in no small part to what author Naomi Klein calls "Disaster Capitalism." Friedman wrote in his 1982 treatise *Capitalism and Freedom*, "When [a] crisis occurs, the actions that are taken depend on the ideas that are lying around."

In Klein's book *The Shock Doctrine*, she explains how immediately after Hurricane Katrina, Friedman used the decimation of New Orleans' infrastructure to push for charter schools, a market-based policy preference of Friedman acolytes. Secretary of Education Arne Duncan was the CEO of Chicago Public Schools at the time, and later described Hurricane Katrina as "the best thing that happened to the education system in New Orleans." Duncan is in the liberal wing of the free market project and a major supporter of charter schools.

There aren't any hurricanes in the Midwest, so how can proponents of privatization like Mayor Rahm Emanuel sell off schools to the highest bidder?

They create a crisis.

Each year, Chicago Public Schools (CPS) projects a billion dollar deficit. The announcement grabs headlines and the Board of Education announces that they must make serious cuts. These cutbacks are never at the top. The Board cuts education programs, after-school activities, and forces more classroom costs onto its employees.

School closings are announced tangentially to the deficit announcement. In years past, the manufactured budget crisis was used as an excuse to lay off teachers. People were fired, class sizes swelled to epic proportions, and — after the budget was reconciled — CPS miraculously found a surplus. This past year's final audited budget showed a surplus of $344 million.

The Chicago Board of Education announced that it must close "underutilized" schools and consolidate students into "receiving schools" to save the district from the projected deficit. The Board argues that some schools simply do not enroll enough students to stay open. A local teacher and parent published ten questions to Chicago Public Schools regarding how much can actually be saved by closing these schools. The Board's responses revolved around the idea that previous administrations have let the problem get so bad they

must act fast and close these schools or else the district will fall over a fiscal cliff — sorry, wrong manufactured crisis. But you get the idea. So now we have a crisis. Schools closed and students shifted around the city. Many of them may have to cross gang territories to get to their receiving schools. School violence spikes. As Rahm Emanuel said in 2008, "You never want a good crisis to go to waste." If only there were a solution "lying around" to attach to this crisis.

At the end of 2012, the Chicago Board of Education approved additional charter schools. The Walton Family Foundation provided seed money for some of these schools. Charter school proliferation can take part of the blame for schools being "underutilized," as they draw students from other schools, but the Board's metric for calculating utilization is also suspect.

Charter schools become the "solution" lying around for parents who want to keep their students close to home in a school that will not be closed the following year. Many charter schools have been infused with additional resources, making their facilities look shiny and new. Parents, through the market-based "choice" system (which is revered by Friedmanites) may enroll their children in these new schools. That is unless their children have special needs, are learning English, or are simply bad at taking tests. Reuters recently published a report that showed how charter schools "cream" students to get the kids they want.

Charter schools that invest heavily in public relations campaigns and receive positive press, but when stacked against magnet schools, which are public schools (staffed by union teachers) with barriers to access, they do not outperform.

Students with special needs, limited English proficiency, or without a regular place to call home are forced to fight over limited resources in the public schools.

This scene is playing out at school closing hearings held by CPS, underwritten by the Walton Family Foundation. School communities are forced to make the case for keeping their schools open. At one meeting on Chicago's north side, schools that take in homeless students from the blighted Uptown community were pitted against schools with programs that address special needs. Some observers likened the scene to the *The Hunger Games*, in which children are forced to fight to the death for the amusement of the 1%.

Our rulers don't bother to stick around and watch the fruits of their policy. But they're more than happy to benefit. The Chicago elites' charter schools are self-perpetuating gifts. The UNO Charter

School Scandal shows how people connected to charters can dole out contracts to friends and family. The UNO network was the recipient of $98 million in state aid to build more schools. The head of UNO, Juan Rangel, was co-chair of Chicago Mayor Rahm Emanuel's election campaign. Members of Rangel's organization are now in the business of installing Illinois state representatives, the very people who hold the purse strings of these state grants. This is the face of the new municipal political machine.

Charter operators generally push back on any efforts of their staffs to unionize. When public schools close and charters open, teachers unions become weaker. Teachers' unions are democratic institutions with ties to the communities they serve. When the public is disempowered, the small patronage army of the mayor becomes more entrenched.

The sale of public schools to charter operators cannot be done slowly. The fast pace of crisis management obscures the graft from the public. UNO specifically needs to operate under these crisis management conditions.

UNO operates under $67,800,000 in outstanding debt. The $98 million state gift cannot be used to pay back this debt because it has been earmarked for capital projects, namely building or improving schools. The only way to keep the UNO patronage train rolling is by continuously expanding and opening schools, with construction contractors serving as potential allies come election time.

The American Enterprise Institute, a conservative think-tank, recently praised this particular brand of charter school. The use of patronage in government hiring was a major argument Friedmanites used for privatizing public services. AEI praises UNO's "assimilationist" philosophy of teaching immigrant youth, so perhaps AEI finds more merit in diluting non-European cultures than in ending patronage. I'm not exactly sure where that fits into the free market orthodoxy, but then again the contradictions in the philosophy far from end there.

Friedmanites often criticize redistributive policies as "picking winners and losers." From the manufactured schools crisis to the market-based solution of charter schools, it appears that the "free market" model picks winners and losers; the winners being the politically connected and the losers being the rest of us.

Assembly Required

The Chicago teachers strike wouldn't have occurred with the internal transformation of the CTU. Here's how it happened.

CORE

History

MICAH UETRICHT

The Chicago Teachers Union has become recognized as vibrant, democratic, and militant in a country where many unions are more likely to be engaged in the organizational equivalent of curling up into the fetal position. Unions have been battered by decades of attacks from big business and both political parties, yet they've been largely unwilling to remake themselves into key players in a broader social movement nor to educate and empower their membership.

But more attention has been paid to the union's recent struggles than how the CTU became the kind of union that it is — one that could take on the right flank of the Democratic Party and free market reformers, go on strike when such a tactic was largely seen as alienating and counterproductive, and lead a movement for educational justice alongside parents and community members in a city long known as an incubator for neoliberal education reform. This transformation was accomplished through the rise of a radical rank-and-file caucus — the Caucus of Rank-and-File Educators (CORE).

History

Chicago is the birthplace of American teacher unionism — Local 1 of the American Federation of Teachers — as well as a historic home of rank-and-file teacher activism stretching back to the early twentieth century. The United Progressive Caucus (UPC) was a part of that history, formed as a combination of several racial justice caucuses by rank-and-file educators of color in the early 1970s. The UPC ran the union nearly uninterrupted from 1972 to 2010, leading the union through five strikes over the course of a decade and a half and winning sizable wage and benefit gains for CTU members — even at times when much of labor was losing ground — due to the leadership's close collaboration with the city's mayors. The caucus's leadership eventually drifted towards narrower goals of improving pay and working conditions for teachers (without engaging significantly with parents and community groups) and a top-down style of governance. Taking up an agenda that could be beneficial to students *and* teachers was nowhere on the table.

As with the rest of the American labor movement, the returns on that strategy eventually disappeared. Economic gains eroded as the city dug its heels in at the bargaining table in the 1990s, demanding concessions and changes that would weaken the union, while power (and pay) remained congealed at the union's top. Similar stories could be found throughout the American labor movement in that era, but the CTU's history of rank-and-file agitation and relatively open internal structures would lead to a successful challenge from liberal educators.

In the 2001 union election, Chicago teachers, fed up with several poor contracts in a row, voted the Proactive Chicago Teachers (PACT) caucus into power, unseating UPC president Tom Reece. Debbie Lynch, an elementary school teacher and longtime UPC critic, ran on a platform of ending corruption within the union, increasing the

union's role in training teachers, and restoring bargaining rights over issues like class sizes that had been lost in the 1990s.

PACT's election brought a shift toward more liberal concerns, but the longtime top-down governing style, with the union's power seen as coming from its shrewd leaders rather than engaged members, remained unchanged. Support for Lynch quickly waned after she, too, negotiated a concessionary contract: teachers ousted her after only one term, reelecting a UPC slate.

As their power and compensation eroded, many Chicago teachers were angry with their union; like any angry electorate, they again tossed the bums out. But like Lynch and Reece, newly elected UPC president Marilyn Stewart also oversaw the negotiation of an unpopular contract in 2007. Membership again rebelled. Some members actually burning copies of the contract outside a press conference after, according to several accounts, Stewart asked for the "yeses" in a contract vote at a House of Delegates meeting, then ran out of the meeting before the "no" vote could be called to declare to reporters that a contract had been settled.

Throughout this period, Chicago teachers expressed their anger by replacing and re-replacing union leaders. But none of the various leadership shifts changed the union's engagement strategy toward members or the broader community. There was no bottom-up approach, centered on the members themselves and allied strongly with a citywide movement for educational justice.

During the union's leadership upheavals, Chicago had become a testing ground for free market education reform. CPS CEO Arne Duncan (now secretary of education under President Obama) and Mayor Richard M. Daley introduced Renaissance 2010, a 2004 program to shut down and "turn around" sixty to seventy schools deemed low-performing and under-utilized by firing the entire staff and converting the majority into charter schools. A small group of rank-and-file teachers began organizing against Renaissance 2010.

Community groups in neighborhoods of color organized against the closures and turnarounds, but the union would not. The leadership appeared resigned to the implementation of free market education reform, still unwilling to mount a fight but continuing to reap the benefits of elected office. Jackson Potter and Jesse Sharkey, history teachers at South and North Side high schools, respectively, took matters into their own hands, making presentations to teachers and community members about the plan, recruiting teachers to join them, and joining the community-led organizing already underway.

They and a growing group of educators attended closure hearings and recruited parents and other teachers for the citywide movement against corporate reform.

The teachers were a loose group hoping to push their leadership to take action, but through organizing alongside community groups, momentum began to build for the teachers to form a formal caucus to run in union elections. Community members were the first to encourage teacher activists to seriously consider running for office. The teachers' deep connections to the organizing initiated by community groups would ultimately legitimize the union in the eyes of community members — they understood the teachers did not simply aim to take power for themselves, but wished to make the union's agenda mutually beneficial for students and teachers alike.

As the organization grew larger, union action against closings remained lackluster. At one point, CTU leadership publicly endorsed a plan designed by Toledo's teachers' union leadership to fire 10 percent of all teachers in the system — confirming to many that working within the existing leadership would get the activist teachers nowhere. Rather than confront free market education reformers, the union's leadership had adopted much of the reformers' rhetoric.

The teachers pushed forward, now calling themselves the Caucus of Rank-and-File Educators (CORE). They held community forums on anti-public education attacks and continued working with community organizations. They held study groups on texts like Naomi Klein's *The Shock Doctrine*, which one staffer described as "a light bulb going off" for teachers. At a nominating convention in August 2009, the caucus chose longtime chemistry teacher Karen Lewis as their presidential candidate. Shortly before the election, CORE organized a massive rally in downtown Chicago with thousands of teachers. Union leadership attempted to take credit, but teachers knew who had organized it. In the May 2010 union elections, CORE triumphed.

Immediately after the news of the victory, president-elect Karen Lewis outlined her and her caucus's vision of a unionism that would confront the forces of neoliberal education reform.

"Corporate America sees K–12 public education as a $380 billion trust that, up until the last ten or fifteen years, they haven't had a sizable piece of," Lewis said. Referencing the CTU's leaders, she

said, "Our union ... didn't point out this simple reality: what drives school reform is a singular focus on profit. Not teaching, not learning — profit." That profit motive would be directly confronted by the union: "This election shows the unity of 30,000 educators standing strong to put business in its place: out of our schools," Lewis said.

Confrontational Stance and Rank-and-File Development

Unlike previous CTU leaderships and the current national union leadership, the CTU under CORE adopted an uncompromisingly confrontational stance against free market education reform. They refused to enter into a partnership with neoliberal Democrats like Mayor Emanuel and foundations like the Gates Foundations, which have used seemingly benevolent nonprofit donations to aggressively pursue a free market agenda in public schools.

CORE also made good on Lewis's campaign promise to "change this into a democratic union responsive to its members" — a transformation that lies at the heart of the union's ability to push for a broad educational justice agenda in Chicago.

The union educated and activated its membership, involving them in an internal democratic process that, for the CTU, was unprecedented. Leadership broadened the rights and responsibilities of members in the governing House of Delegates, and fourteen member-led committees were tasked with central roles in the union's day-to-day functioning. Contract committees were set up at each school, and each committee member was responsible for communicating with ten other educators face-to-face, including school employees like cafeteria workers who were members of other unions.

The creation of an organizing department, which had never before existed in the union, was one of the most crucial changes CORE instituted. The department was tasked with continued organizing alongside community groups and expanding the union's work with community members. Through it, the CTU transformed itself from a service-model union — where the union's primary purpose is to provide services for their members like representing them in grievances against school management — to a union where the staff's principal task is facilitating the development of members so they can be at the helm of the union themselves and advance a broadly progressive agenda, in tandem with organized communities.

The difference could be seen in the way union members began interacting with parents. In one school on the Northwest Side, for example, CPS administration attempted to co-locate a charter school in the same building as a middle school. In past years, according to union organizer Matt Luskin, the union would have mounted a legal battle with CPS to halt the co-location and hoped for the best; the fight would have been largely in the union's hands rather than parents' and teachers'. But CTU staff "encouraged the teachers themselves to take control of the situation by organizing with parents," Luskin says. Teachers and parents organized together to reach out to other schools in the neighborhood, meeting with their Local School Councils, democratically elected bodies of parents and community members in every Chicago school. Eventually, they held a protest opposing the charter's opening that drew several hundred people.

"The parents didn't see themselves as particularly anti-charter school, or even pro-union, on the front end," Luskin says. But parents realized the charter's construction would interrupt their children's school, and, once built, the charter would undercut their neighborhood school. "And then by the end of it, they were very anti-charter and very pro-union."

In another case, three elementary teachers worked closely with parents around increasing special education funding for their children, pointing out potential violations of laws around special ed students. The school's principal, threatened by such agitation that cast her management in a poor light, gave unsatisfactory ratings to all three teachers — putting their future teaching careers in serious jeopardy.

"In the past," Luskin says, "the union would have said, 'Well, you can file a grievance'" — leaving the teachers to passively await the outcome while union staff handled the fight. Instead, teachers organized house meetings with parents, who strongly supported the teachers. Soon, the teachers accompanied a group of forty parents to a meeting of the Local School Council to issue an official rebuke of the principal. The teachers' ratings were eventually restored, and the principal transferred to another school.

The union's organizing department also trained rank-and-file members in organizing tactics and educated them on the city's major public policy issues. Members of the House of Delegates, the union's representative body of teachers, received training in "bread-and-butter" issues like enforcing the contract's provisions, but also subjects beyond the classroom like fighting school closures. The department started a summer internship organizing program where teachers learned about the city's tax increment financing (TIF) program, a shadowy financing scheme controlled by the mayor that has been used to divert public funds from public institutions like schools and libraries to major corporations in the city. The teachers then knocked on educators' doors across the city, teaching them about TIF.

Central to the CTU's success have been the centrality of rank-and-file members increasingly carrying out the union's work and their organizing with parents for a mutually beneficial agenda. The former helped lead to 90 percent of all CTU members voting to strike and a city awash in red-shirted CTU educators during the strike; the latter helped lead to overwhelming numbers of public school parents and the Chicago population as a whole siding with the teachers during the strike rather than Mayor Emanuel.

Through a radical caucus of rank-and-file teachers in strong partnership with community organizations, the CTU became a totally different kind of union. That transformation was years in the making — indicating that there probably are not any shortcuts to building the kind of fighting union the CTU has become in the last few years. No teachers would have walked off the job, shut down downtown Chicago in a sea of 30,000 strikers and supporters, or confronted the neoliberal consensus on education without years of patient internal organizing and educating. And if that organizing had remained limited to Chicago educators, rather than being rooted in community-based fights by parents and community members against free market education reform, the union would never have been able to successfully fight back.

The 2012 strike was a victory for the teachers and against free market reform, but the Chicago Public Schools have still suffered. The contract negotiated during the strike contained numerous concessions (though less than the Board of Education wanted). Yet immediately after the strike, Mayor Emanuel and the Board of Education ignored massive public protest and shut down 50 schools, the largest spate of school closures in American history. And a crushing round of budget cuts swept the district this summer as the district switched to per-pupil funding — leading to $162 million in classroom-level budget cuts and over 3,000 teacher layoffs.

Rank-and-file caucuses like CORE aren't panaceas for all that ails Chicago teachers and students, of course. But teachers should look to Chicago for some ideas about how to transform their unions. Fending off the attacks on public education will require more than new faces in union leadership — it will take a transformation from the bottom up that fosters genuine alliances with community members and parents.

The grievance process, imperfect as it is, can be used to challenge management and invigorate union locals.

Grieve to Win

KEVIN PROSEN

F iling a grievance is the most rudimentary form of union activity and representation in the workplace.

A grievance is filed when a union member feels that management or administration has violated one of the principles of their contract. For many workers, it is their first experience in organized workplace confrontation. To the union staffer, the grievance is often the most important way that unions advocate for their members at the level of the "shop floor." For workers experienced with the process, however, it can feel like a kind of cruel trick; grievances linger sometimes for years without even checking a boss's behavior. Often no resolution is ever achieved. Despite the shortcomings of the grievance process, it can be a useful tool for educators looking to invigorate their union chapter, when conducted with the kind of solidarity and élan typically lacking from narrow discussions of contract interpretation and arbitration settlements.

The grievance system itself emerged as part of the post–World War II system of labor-capital relations that solidified "business unionism" as a bulwark against the pre-war period's more radical forms of labor struggle. It allows for management to channel workers' discontent into less threatening channels than the strike waves of the depression and those immediately following World War II. Union staff and bureaucracies ballooned across all industries in order to manage the new apparatus of "shopfloor jurisprudence." Such a system, whatever the surface symmetries between labor and management, inevitably favored employers.

Labor scholar Kim Moody describes the way bosses exploited this system:

> [M]anagement could remove an issue from the shopfloor to a higher level simply by denying any grievance at the first step or two of the procedure. Grievances then piled up at higher stages

and were either arbitrated if they were regarded as important by higher levels of the union or bargained away at contract time. As a consequence of the time-delay inherent in the system, management initiatives, even when blatantly in violation of the contract, could not be stopped through the grievance procedure.

This will sound familiar to anybody working in a modern teachers' union. Such time delays have the effect of dampening organization and action on the "shop floor" and creating immense frustration among the membership, while allowing management prerogatives to continue unabated. The grievance process can also be used by administration as a form of bargaining by force, wherein management can try to press on ambiguous parts of the contract in the hope of obtaining an arbitration decision in their favor.

In his 1973 pamphlet "Toward Teacher Power," Steve Zeluck wrote of this process: "Thus the board may decide to openly violate a clause (especially if it is in the least bit ambiguous). This is done only partly as a 'testing' operation. For if the union takes the grievance to arbitration, there is, on the average, at least a 50-50 chance

of losing." Indeed, many grievances stall before arbitration, since the unions are only willing to bring ones they're certain they'll win. In opposition to this unsatisfying resolution mechanism, Zeluck proposed alternative courses of direct action on the job site: "group refusal to perform extra-curricular duties; voluntary duties, coaching duties, sick-outs, demonstrations, etc."

Such propositions are music to the ears of many union militants, although they sound like anachronistic advice when many of our co-workers are terrified to put their name on a petition to their principal or grieve even the most flagrant contract violations. Often teachers are more willing to pursue individual solutions; "playing along" and "staying off the radar" replace concerted action and militancy. Zeluck was writing in the early seventies after a period of sustained teacher militancy, including illegal strikes which had given birth to modern teacher unionism in many cities.

Present-day teachers have nothing approaching this experiential basis from which to draw courage. Fear, anxiety, and individual solutions have replaced solidarity and concerted action. While exciting new forms of rank-and-file defiance have started to emerge — like the boycott of standardized testing at Garfield High School in Seattle last year — such examples remain exceptions to the general rule.

How do we get from here to there? What can teachers do to break down fear and apathy in the workplace and lay a basis for more daring forms of struggle that will be necessary to confront corporate education reform? Since it is "within the system" and not outside it, organizing a grievance campaign in your school can be a useful transitional step toward more confrontational forms of action. Rather than placing faith in the grievance and arbitration system, rank-and-file teachers need to make the grievance machine work for them. We grieve not because we believe in the process, but to prepare the groundwork to transcend it in the future.

Grievances as a form of workplace action are not without certain distinct advantages. Once freed from the narrow bureaucratic concerns of what is most likely to win at an arbitration table, the grievance becomes a useful way to educate, agitate, and organize, as the old mantra goes. The important thing is to infuse the process with a sense of collective action, that forgotten key to effective unionism. Because it pertains to specific contract articles, the grievance provides an opportunity to train staff to read and interpret the contract, a skill which does not come naturally to anyone and which the unions do not, unfortunately, cultivate among the general membership. Since teachers are often scared of administrative retaliation for sticking their necks out, conducting a grievance collectively can teach a basic lesson about the power of solidarity.

Activists should identify issues that affect the entire staff or an entire department; there's safety and strength in numbers. This could be the allocation of per-session jobs, abuse of non-teaching assignments, forced overtime, micromanagement, or any other issue large or small that affects large numbers of people on your staff. If the particular grievance isn't covered by the contract, file it anyway as a letter of protest or complaint to the principal, rather than as a formal grievance. Once you've freed yourself from the concerns of winning at some uncertain future at the arbitration table and committed yourself to asserting strength in the workplace, there's no need to be bound by what is "contractual."

Train a layer of collaborators on the staff in the specific grounds for the grievance, and how to engage with staff members' hesitations and doubts. Be sure to talk to every staff member and check them off as they sign. Having more than one person circulating the grievance helps show that it is a collective process, and not the work of a rogue crank. When the principal schedules the "Step One" meeting, bring all the signatories into the office together, no matter how many there are. Show that the staff is united.

Successful campaigns like this can alter the school environment, even if they don't "win" in the narrow terms afforded by the grievance process. For the staff, they can produce a sense of collective strength and solidarity that can break down the isolation of the classroom experience and the divisive pressures at play in the school system. It can also compel administration to be more conflict-avoidant, and seek more collaborative ways to resolve potential problems with the staff rather than against them. This is the most basic and elemental level of workplace power, one that has been conceded long ago in countless schools across the country.

Most contemporary teachers' unions lack militancy, membership solidarity, and even a meaningful connection with rank-and-file educators. A thoughtful, well-organized grievance campaign can help build unions at the most important level, in the schools. Such organization is the precondition for turning the tide of education reform. It would be a small step, but one in the right direction.

Reorienting teachers' unions to be vehicles for change will require engaging new members and pre-service teachers.

Mentoring for Mobilization

ADAM HEENAN

Like the vast majority of workers today, I was not raised in a union family. I learned what a union can bring to the job, and about union democracy and decision making in the Caucus of Rank and File Educators and the Chicago Teachers Union (CTU) House of Delegates. From mentors and colleagues, I learned what it meant to apply these ideals to my teaching craft and identity. Now I am seeking out new educators to mentor so we can improve our public schools.

Over the past four years, I have developed outreach for new and incoming union members in my school and in pre-service teacher programs. I have also used outreach opportunities to talk with pre-service teachers on and off campus, engaging them with questions that matter to them and the principle that matters to us all: dignity for students and teachers in the classroom.

If we are to reorient our teachers' unions to be both participatory and transformative — as well as provide new members with a toolkit to resist corporate-style education reform — we must be more strategic in collectively engaging new members and pre-service teachers. In order to accomplish this, we must use the formal structure and resources of our union and our grassroots organizing skills as union sisters and brothers teaching in the classroom down the hall.

The Need

Over the past thirty years and across all sectors, union membership has steeply declined and with it, workplace quality and worker compensation. Teachers aren't wholly exempt from this trend, but we are still the most unionized profession in the United States. This is part of the reason for the well organized attack on teachers' unions. Conservatives and neoliberals attack unions not only to dilute our political and financial power, but also to develop a compliant and unquestioning workforce, unwilling to challenge initiatives that are harmful to educators and students.

It's not enough to tell our young members to "study your union history." Rather, telling our new members to "go study" would have the opposite effect. It's dismissive, and potentially deleterious to the goal of organizing new members. I compare it to telling my history students to respect history solely by reading about it. Whenever I teach my students that way, they disengage and feel disrespected. We can expect first-year educators and new members to respond the same way.

Similar to good professional development, any new member engagement strategy must offer both support and opportunities for autonomy. A new member engagement plan should be informative, supportive, inclusive, transformative, and ultimately self-sustaining. The goal is not only to educate, but also to empower members and humanize unions and unionism.

Outreach

It makes the most sense to engage pre-service teachers in discussions before they enter the classroom. There are very practical reasons for this, not the least of which is that corporate education reform groups like Teach for America, Students for Education Reform (organized by Democrats for Education Reform), and StudentsFirst are already doing outreach on college campuses. The National Education Association has student chapters which vary in their degree of activity, but club members often describe it as insurance protection for when one starts student teaching. Chapters rarely host discussions, speakers, or events that are historically grounded or offer a union perspective.

Teachers and their unions must be more intentional in how we educate and organize incoming members. Union locals must consider ways in which they can strategically develop relationships with schools of education to sponsor events and activities that allow for pre-service teachers to access both union leadership and rank-and-file members.

Outreach that is structured in this way can clarify questions and develop young members' political agency. Even among locals where this may be difficult or cost prohibitive, we can encourage and support our rank-and-file members to do outreach to their former schools of education on their own. This form of organizing can be as empowering for members as for the young people they speak to or meet at events.

At the very least, we must do outreach to pre-service teachers when they enter our buildings for credentialing and student teach-

ing. If we are the first connection they have to teacher unionism, what can we do to address their many concerns about the profession they are about to enter?

The most basic questions might not be the most interesting, but they are the most urgent, and when we are not helpful in answering new members' most immediate concerns, we risk complete disengagement. Young teachers often want answers to questions longtime educators may take for granted: What is a union? Who is part of a union? How is it organized? How does a union operate? What is a contract? What is tenure and how is it different from seniority?

Each semester I teach an after-school seminar called Unionism 101 for all the credentialing teachers placed in my building. Central to the seminar is a new member welcoming kit I use to help explain unions' functions, membership, and structure. I usually include a copy of the most recent contract, current legislation to watch, a Frequently Asked Questions page, and a leadership and decision-making flow chart (which also describes how the individual member is situated within the union). I also explicitly invite seminar participants to the next publicized union action, and ask them to bring their friends and colleagues.

Support Through Mentorship

Nearly half of the educators who enter the profession leave after five years, according to the researchers David Perda and Richard Ingersoll. Many cite the lack of support. This is something the union can easily provide, by connecting new educators to veterans. Many unions already have in place mentor-mentee pairing for new members, and participation is crucial for developing agency.

Unions should offer choices for mentors and mentees, such as the "speed-dating" model, or partnership building, in which participants get to know many mentors and mentees in a social setting and list preferences based upon wants, needs, and affinity with other participants. Under these circumstances, mentees have a better chance to develop a supporting relationship with an experienced educator-unionist rather than if someone was chosen for them without any input.

Mentoring, when done well, can also help combat implicit and overt ageism, sexism, and racism among members, further strengthening the capacity of educators to work together towards common goals. It's especially important to combat ageism, because there is an oft-perceived rift between newer members and more experienced members. However, this is most often due to structures that encourage ageism and diminish all teachers' ability to recognize and develop solidarity despite differences. Young members may also come in to the profession with a belief that they know what teaching is and doubt they can learn from educators who have been in the classroom for years. Supportive mentorship creates conditions of empathy and empowerment between generations of educators who want what is best for the profession and the people engaged in it.

Socialize in Order to Mobilize

To be attractive to young members, unions need to be accessible, flexible, and responsive. This requires a shift in unionism from the service and organizing model to what I call the engagement model of unionism.

Chicago teachers have creatively incorporated varying interests into their union. To name a few: The AFT Alliance of Charter Teachers and Staff Local 4343 running club, civic and cultural parade participation (floats and marches), the CTU Motorcycle Riders Club, and teacher-artist galleries. Social activities allow educators to connect their professional identities to their personal lives, and young members begin to see the union as part of their identity. This can help tear down perceived barriers between union brothers and sisters.

Young members must see unions as relevant and valuable, or unionism will perish. The goal cannot simply be to engage new teachers for reasons of political action or financial sustainability, however. New teachers will see through this shallow approach. But if young members see unions as vehicles for democratic decision-making and an improved quality of life — for themselves and their students — then they'll have a deeper involvement and commitment.

We must allow and encourage young teachers to participate and transform unions in new and creative ways. This will take certain flexibility on the part of union leadership, which is often prone to inertia. But it's the only option. Continued inflexibility and lack of engagement with new members will quicken the death of teachers' union locals across the country.

Chicago teachers have been peerless in resisting the international push for education privatization and marketization.

Changing the World in One Contract

LOIS WEINER

U rging the suspension of their fall 2012 strike, Chicago Teachers Union President Karen Lewis said Chicago teachers couldn't change the world in one contract. She was wrong. While there were important items the union didn't win, the strike electrified teachers around the world, inspiring a reinvigorated labor presence in the Windy City.

The reform leadership of the CTU has shown teachers that for their professional knowledge to be respected, they must fight for it to be so. Try as the media did to cast the strike as being a traditional labor dispute about pay, they couldn't make a convincing case to Chicago parents. Because of the union's morally essential (and strategically sound) embedding of economic demands in a framework for truly improving the schools, parents understood that teachers were on the side of their children.

Chicago schools have a unique history, and what occurred there won't be so readily duplicated in other US cities. Teacher unionism was born in Chicago a century ago, under the leadership of a socialist elementary school teacher, Margaret Haley. The city's schools also saw serious contestation by parents for voice in running their schools through local school councils. The teachers' union, too, has been different from most big locals in having reformers win office — in contrast to cities like New York.

Still, this strike has changed the political equation, not only here in the US but internationally. With the exception of a few Nordic holdouts like Finland, schools are being privatized and curriculum reduced to preparation for standardized tests, globally. This is an international project to make schooling serve the interests of transnational corporations. Chicago teachers have shown that a union leadership with a vision and courage, one that empowers its members, can turn back some of the most pernicious elements of this global project.

One telling aspect of the strike is that the media and the politicians totally missed what was brewing. The story actually began when the Caucus of Rank and File Educators organized school by school and swept the old guard out of office. Their program was precisely the one on which this strike was waged. Yet their victory went unnoticed in the national media and by conservatives and liberals alike — including progressive publications like *The Nation*.

What has occurred in the past decade is that Democrats and Republicans alike are captives of their own ideology and their exquisitely orchestrated propaganda. They are in thrall to what an April 1999 Merrill Lynch report describes as the "new mindset," of schools being "retail outlets" and the school board a "customer service department." Their belief is that schools, students, and teachers will improve when they are subject to the "discipline of the market." Since their mind is set, nothing that teachers, parents, or students say alters their beliefs. It takes teachers and parents shutting down a school system to get through to them.

As it turns out, the market's "discipline" is no more effective in improving schools than it is in making banks responsible. What Chicago teachers have shown the world is that teachers' unions have the potential to lead a movement that will take back our schools.

DISSENT STANDS WITH TEACHERS

Follow ongoing coverage of the fight for public education on **Belabored**, *Dissent*'s biweekly podcast about work and unions, hosted by labor journalists Sarah Jaffe and Michelle Chen.

On Belabored's first episode we interviewed CTU President Karen Lewis. More than 100 episodes later, we've talked with teachers from across the country—not to mention scholars, writers, and organizers including Ai-jen Poo, Adolph Reed, Micah Uetricht, and Megan Erickson.

Find Belabored on iTunes, Stitcher, or Soundcloud. And join the conversation on Twitter using #Belabored.

dissentmagazine.org/belabored

CORE's Coming
Out Party

KAREN LEWIS

In 2006, I left the largest high school in Chicago — Lane Tech, a selective enrollment high school with a diverse student body — for another selective enrollment school, King, with a predominantly African-American population.

Still a high school chemistry teacher, my work at Lane as a delegate to the Chicago Teachers Union's governing body, the House of Delegates, brought me into deep conflict with the principal, who I felt was a bully, unethical, and hypocritical. While he was never able to retaliate against me, he went after my closest friends and colleagues. My sense of fair play and defense of fellow union members had taken its toll. So I left, without looking back.

When I got to King, the delegate (with whom I had served on the Executive Board) wanted some support; I, however, wanted to keep a low profile. But she had won election to the executive board of PACT (Pro-Active Caucus of Teachers and School Employees), a reform caucus that challenged the stranglehold the UPC (United Progressive Caucus) had on CTU leadership. I joined PACT in 2001 — the same year the caucus won the election and took control of the union.

When the contract then-president Debbie Lynch negotiated initially failed to pass a vote by union membership, the final contract was relentlessly used to attack her. In 2004, when PACT lost to the "New UPC," the high school functional vice-presidents of PACT, including me, won seats on the union's executive board.

My time there was, to say the least, depressing. PACT members were isolated and not allowed to participate in real union governance. The union's executive board meetings were dry-run rehearsals for carrying out the UPC leadership's will at forthcoming House of Delegate meetings and were a complete waste of time and energy. There was no strategy for moving the union forward; for fighting against then–Chicago Public Schools CEO Arne Duncan's "Renaissance 2010," the plan for closing schools and opening charter, contract, and performance schools (and the precursor to the Obama administration's Race to the Top program).

Instead of communicating a plan to move the union in a different direction, the UPC seemed to focus on ensuring their re-election. They spent House of Delegates meetings complaining about why they could not do anything for members except win slam dunk grievances (primarily related to payroll, when principals tried to make people work for free). They had successfully attacked Lynch and her contract and ensured their re-election in 2007, but they did not appear to have much of a plan for the union beyond that.

By then, I thought I was done with the union. I was disappointed that neither the old guard UPC nor the supposed reformers in PACT were able to clearly articulate the nature of corporate school reform and build resistance among the membership. I had planned to retire in 2008, but my transfer to King made teaching joyous again, so I decided to postpone the decision.

Once of the best parts of working with PACT was building relationships with people I respected. So when union member Debby Pope told me that another member, Jesse Sharkey, was starting a new caucus, I agreed to attend a meeting. As my husband and I trudged up three flights of stairs on an unseasonably warm evening in April 2008 for a meeting at the Casa Aztlan community center, I could see this caucus was going to be very different.

There were familiar faces around the table — Carol Caref, Norine Gutenkanst, Jesse Sharkey, Debby Pope, and George Schmidt — but also, impressively, young, fresh faces — Jackson Potter, Kenzo Shibata, Nate Goldbaum, Kyle Westbrook. Jesse chaired the first meeting, focusing on questions like, "How do we resist policies that harm our students?" "How do we fight the school closings?"

We were given an article by education policy professor Pauline Lipman which analyzed the "Mid-South Plan," an urban renewal scheme hatched by the elite pro-business Civic Committee of the Commercial Club — the architects of "Renaissance 2010." While they claimed the plan was to improve education, its true intention was a long-term real estate plan, a land grab by closing public schools and forcing poor and working-class people out of the city. All the signs were there, if we had simply paid attention. My husband and I joined the Caucus of Rank-and-File Educators (CORE) on the spot.

CORE continued to pay attention. Shared responsibility and deep discussions with parent, student, and community voices on how to push the CTU in a direction meant that we had to think about our union in a very different way. CORE members went to every school closing hearing, every charter school opening, and every Board of Education meeting, where we identified ourselves as members of CORE and made clear that we opposed the city's education policies that destroyed neighborhoods and harmed our children.

In January 2009, we called for a citywide meeting on the future of public education in Chicago at Malcolm X College. By then, we had engaged CTU leadership, several community organizations, and the educators' group Teachers for Social Justice, as well as teachers who had been displaced through school closings or turnarounds and teachers whose schools were targeted for closure.

That Saturday morning, a blizzard descended on Chicago. The union's field representatives, members of the UPC sent to observe the proceedings and size CORE up, sat together and smugly looked at us upstarts, thinking the likelihood of people trudging through a Chicago winter morning to attend a meeting on education reform was next to nil. Yet slowly, union members and community members started trickling in; some schools sent busloads of people. The looks on the union staffers' faces turned from self-satisfaction to awe. How had they so miscalculated?

The January 2009 Educational Summit was CORE's coming-out party. By then, CTU's UPC leadership was in tatters; by May 2010, five caucuses vied for leadership. Only one talked about the need to include our natural allies in the struggle against educational apartheid and the takeover of Chicago's public schools by the city's ruling class; only one had been organizing alongside those allies for years; and only one had begun laying the groundwork for the strike that would come in September 2012. That caucus was CORE.